I0030261

Testimonials

Bernard manages to find the right balance between learning without posturing and facilitating with flexibility. He covers difficult topics with humility and humour. The experience he creates feels intuitive and becomes an evolution of learning as opposed to delivering a pre-determined program. Each learning opportunity has a bespoke feeling that leads to high engagement and exponential learning.

David Longman, Managing Director, Diversified Communications, Australia

I credit Bernard with helping us transform our business from a 'good' company to a 'great' company. He has helped us to understand where we are as a leadership team and what we need to do to take us from a functional team to a flourishing leadership team.

Diego Ascani, CEO Sedgwick, Australia

Bernard has helped us mould a newly formed, first-class group of individuals into a seamless leadership team, collectively accountable for decision-making and speedier cross functional working in a high growth business.

Jane McNally, CEO Camilla

Bernard has helped us, as a leadership team, to understand and commit to teaming better together. Bernard helped us create a safe space to discuss the undiscussables through developing a culture of openness and trust with a clear team purpose and values set.

Karen McGoldrick, Vice President and Managing Director, Invisalign, ANZ

We engaged with Bernard to unlock the potential in our leadership team that will see us shift from being a highly 'functional' team into the state of 'flourishing'. Bernard has energised us all through bravely restating our team purpose. Like elite athletes, we are setting out on the journey of shaving off milliseconds on our personal bests to take us to a whole new level.

Stacey Tomasoni, Managing Director, Datacom CONNECT

The growth of the team through Bernard's direction and guidance has been measurable and has allowed the team to grow the quality outcomes of our business. I would recommend Bernard to organisations looking to take a good team who is 'delivering' to an exceptional team who is 'high performing'.

Toby Long, General Manager, NSW Residential, Mirvac

Without doubt, the most tangible improvement is the level of conversations and the quality of performance has improved and matured considerably. There's now a shared focus of business improvement and it's about working together and helping each other to achieve this. As a result, the positive impact on our bottom line is inevitable.

Sean Dempsey, CEO Plan Partners

Coming to identify the executive team's purpose as, *We Unlock Possibilities*, has served to focus our collective capability to achieve our 2020 strategy and beyond.

Mike Salisbury, CEO McMillan Shakespeare Group

Team Better Together

TEAM
BETTER
TOGETHER

5 disciplines of high performing teams

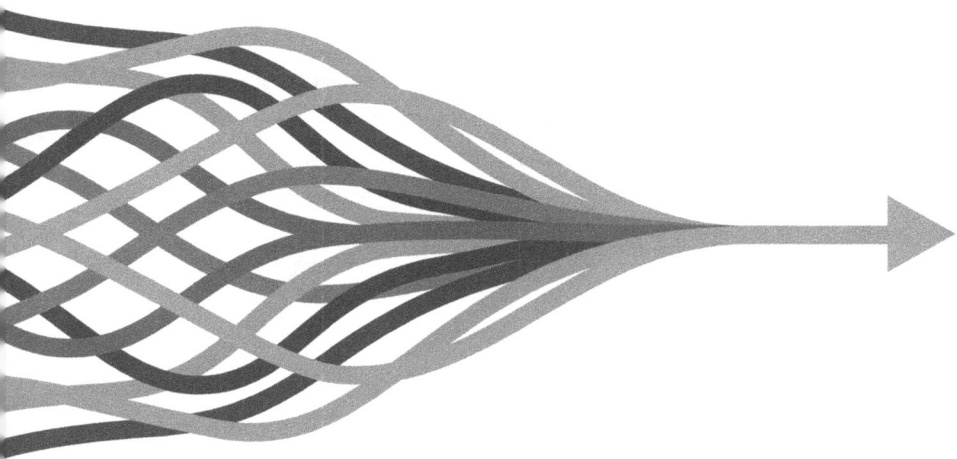

BERNARD DESMIDT

Copyright © Bernard Desmidt

All models copyright © Bernard Desmidt

First published in 2021 in Melbourne, Australia

ISBN: 978-0-6453624-0-4 (pbk) eISBN: 978-0-6453624-1-1

A catalogue record for this book is available
from the National Library of Australia

Edited by Joanna Yardley at The Editing House

Typeset, bound and printed in Australia by BookPOD

All rights reserved. No part of this publication may be reproduced
by any means without the prior written consent of the publisher.

Every effort has been made to trace (and seek permission for use
of) the original source of material used within this book. Where the
attempt has been unsuccessful, the publisher would be pleased
to hear from the author/publisher to rectify any omission.

A catalogue record for this
book is available from the
NATIONAL
LIBRARY   National Library of Australia
OF AUSTRALIA

Contents

Part Four: What is happening

Part Five: Making it happen

Part Six: Team coaching (program)

Preface

*'What we learn is useful to us. What
we share is useful to the world.'*
—Matt Church, Founder of the Thought Leaders Business School

This book is for team leaders, whether you are a CEO or managing director of an organisation, the general manager of a business unit, the head of a functional team or a project team leader. It is a practical guide to help leaders unlock the power within their teams and harness the collective capacity and capability to achieve the greatest things possible.

This book comes at a time of unprecedented change, where leaders need to adopt new ways of thinking, being and doing. Our ways of navigating complexity and uncertainty have changed forever. The hybrid ways of working have set a new order. Now, *our way of work* is as important as *our place of work*.

An organisation's success is dependent upon creating high performance teams where connection, collaboration and coordination flow between and within—together and apart. Teams are the predominant unit of organisational performance; nothing of value and impact can be achieved without teaming.

This book is the result of a 20-year corporate career where I worked as a leader and member of numerous teams in different industries within multinational companies in many countries across the world. Although the common theme was an inherent potential to access and harness the collective capacity and capability, it happened very rarely.

My journey to pursuing a career as an executive and team coach inspired me to write this book.

Acknowledgements

Over the years, I have worked with many leadership teams who honoured me with trust as we navigated towards a common end along an untraveled road. Their courage and commitment to learning is commendable. They accessed deeper levels of individual and collective resourcefulness, and achieved unimaginable change and significant accomplishments. Above all, their journeys enabled them to live and lead with greater fulfilment and impact.

To Kim, Lee and Guy, thank you for your unconditional love and selflessness that makes it possible for me to continue to do work I love and with people I like in the way I want.

Thank you to Sheila Westhuizen, my business manager, for your infinite capacity and capability to make my life easier.

I am humbled to be part of the Thought Leaders Business School. You are a community of some of the brightest minds whose generosity, encouragement and support made this book possible. Thank you to the 'Fabulous Five' who held me accountable to the last sentence.

My work has been made possible thanks to the many thought leaders who have travelled this road before me and who have guided me to find my pathway in service of others. There are too many to mention but my deepest appreciation goes to

Peter Hawkins, Jon Katzenbach, Alan Sieler, Patrick Lencioni and John Kotter.

To my editor, Jo Yardley, thank you for your patience and professionalism in helping my thoughts become accessible.

To my book designer, Sylvie Blair, thank you for bringing the book to life.

This book is born of my commitment to live a life by design consistent with my personal mission statement (1994):

I will be guided by my personal mission statement and I will share it. I will strive never to 'blow out' others' candles but will make it my responsibility to light many throughout my life. I will hold in high regard experience and opportunity, love and care, and knowledge and growth in abundance.

I will focus my efforts on the important matters: my health, family and work. In doing so, I will be a loving partner and father; I will be honest and truthful to myself and others; and I will care for others and the environment.

I will strike a balance in my life. I will exercise regularly, eat healthily, grow in knowledge and give myself fully to all my relationships with others.

I will maintain the habit of listening to understand rather than to be understood by others. I will hold others with respect, dignity and legitimacy despite how similar or different their views may be to mine. I will be curious and open to learning with and from others.

I will retain a positive self-image and belief in myself.

At the end of my life, I will be remembered for having lived out my personal mission.

To the greatest team ever.

Thank you Kim, Lee and Guy for your endless love.

About the author

Bernard Desmidt enables organisations to become leader-full. As an accomplished coach, facilitator, speaker and author, he helps leaders become their best selves so they can live and lead with greater fulfilment and impact.

His expertise is to unlock the power in teams and access the collective capacity and capability to achieve the greatest things possible.

Bernard has delivered more than 20,000 hours of executive and team coaching and has facilitated leadership development programs across Australia and internationally.

His first book, *Inside-Out Leadership: How to Master the 4 Principles of Effective Leadership and Become the Leader Others Choose to Follow*, is a must-read for leaders committed to differentiating themselves and evolving their leadership to meet the demands of today's increasingly complex and uncertain world.

Dr Marshall Goldsmith (recognised as the world's #1 leadership thinker) endorsed the book:

'*Inside-Out Leadership* is laden with common sense. Leaders will read this book and wonder why they're not already doing this.'

'We live in a culture of hyper-individualism. There is always a tension between self and society, between the individual and the group. Over the past sixty years we have swung too far toward the self. The only way out is to rebalance, to build a culture that steers people toward relation, community, and commitment—the things we most deeply yearn for, yet undermine with our hyper-individualistic way of life.'

The Second Mountain by David Brooks

Introduction

I emigrated from South Africa in January 2000 with my life partner, Kim, and our two young children, Lee and Guy. Neither of us had a job but we had committed to restarting our lives. We estimated we had enough money to survive for six months once we converted our total wealth from South African rand to Australian dollars.

After three months, I secured an executive role with an IT and telecommunications distributor – part of a wholly owned subsidiary of a global organisation. In the early 2000s, the distribution sector was going through a radical technological evolution. Amazon was five years old and its presence and power were felt. Remaining viable, given the high volume / low margin nature of the distribution sector, meant investing in the automation of the 'picking and packing' components of the distribution process. Distributors had to find ways to reduce their cost of sales—the sector had to automate to not only reduce costs but increase efficiencies.

System failures, process breakdowns and industrial action had a significant impact on distributors' ability to meet service level agreements and provide the guarantees manufacturers required to deliver their products into the market.

This was my first role working in Australia and as a member of the executive team, I had much to unlearn to adapt and assimilate to the 'Australian way'. I found much of it confusing.

For one, I did not understand why everyone called each other 'mate' when it was clear that some were far from being mates. It took time to understand that the context in which others called one another mate mattered most. Mate could mean anything from friend to foe.

However, I found it most difficult to deal with how my colleagues chose to avoid talking about the 'elephant in the room' but rather would talk about the 'elephant outside of the room'.

It soon became apparent that the executive team was a group of stars but far from being a star team. Much of the team members' energy and focus was on competing among themselves for a share of voice, value and vanity. On the surface it appeared to be a functional team; in reality, it was floundering.

It was floundering because of the varied and misaligned perspectives among team members of what we thought our stakeholders expected of us. At the time, our parent company was looking to divest of its global interests in IT&T distribution, while our customers were looking to us to invest in more efficient systems and processes, and lower the distribution costs to protect their eroding profit margins due to competitive pressures.

The team floundered because it lacked a common purpose—it was a group of individuals rather than a cohesive and unified team. Upon inviting the team to reflect on its purpose, the default response was 'to meet our stakeholders' expectations'. Despite not knowing our stakeholders' expectations, the default response had more to do with *what* we did, rather than *why* we existed as a team.

Most concerning were the dysfunctional relationships born out of levels of distrust and disrespect of others' differing views and opinions. More was unsaid for fear of disagreeing with the predominant view. Team members wouldn't express their concerns with the person involved. Decisions were made without prior consultations which meant meetings were futile.

While I was part of this team, I found myself looking to others as the cause and reason for the dysfunctionality. This was easy to do until one day I asked myself, 'How am I contributing to the dysfunctionality in ways I am not seeing?' I had not realised that I was behaving no differently to my colleagues. How I experienced them was how they experienced me.

By acknowledging this truth, I had only one question to ask myself, 'What responsibility do I have to myself and each team member to address the situation?'

At the next monthly executive team meeting, I was committed to raising the 'elephant in the room'. I felt an overwhelming force come over me and I thumped my fists on the table out of frustration and irritation. It was too late. *What had I done,* I thought? *How could I be so unprofessional*? The meeting room turned silent and all eyes focused on me. But I knew they understood what made me act that way—as a team, we all knew: what we think is not what we say, what we feel is not what we name and what we say is not what we mean.

The CEO turned to me and said, 'so, Bernard, where do we go from here?' A month later we engaged the help of an executive team coach …

… and that is where my story began.

WHAT'S COMING UP IN *TEAM BETTER TOGETHER*

Achieving lasting and transformational behavioural change requires three modes of learning:

1. **Team building** to enable team members to get to know and understand each other so they can **form** together.

2. **Team development** to **inform** the team about the processes, systems and practices that are essential for working efficiently and effectively together.

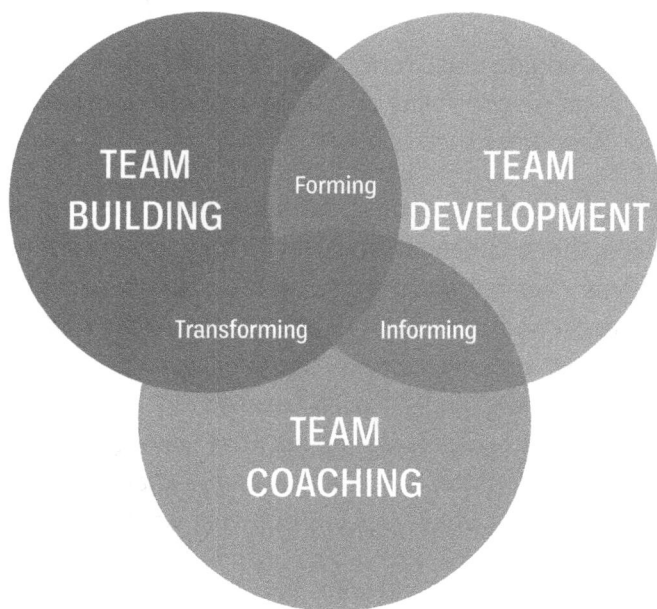

3. **Team coaching** to enable teams to **transform** by seeing things differently and accessing new possibilities to access and leverage the team's collective capacity

and capability. In our complex and interdependent world with its increasing pace and volatility of change, leadership goes beyond individuals and requires more effective collective leadership. This requires leadership teams to learn, to see things differently, and to adapt and adjust. This book focuses on how teams can transform themselves and how organisations can succeed by creating a culture of teamwork to secure their most competitive advantage.

At its essence, this book highlights subtle distinctions with a significant impact on accessing the power within teams. What is sometimes obvious to do can be difficult to accomplish. This book is about making the obvious more accessible, applicable and achievable.

Above all else, this book helps leaders create high performing teams by answering these questions:

1. Is the team a group of leaders or a leadership team? What should it be?

2. Why does the team exist and how aligned is the team to a common purpose?

3. What needs to change in how the team members engage and relate together? What ways of working will enable the team to flourish?

4. What collective goals is the team accountable for and which can only be achieved by working interdependently?

5. How effectively do members learn with and from each other? How effectively do members grow and evolve as a team?

6. What would it take to transition a team to become a flourishing, high performing team? What does a coaching experience need to involve to help achieve this?

As a team member (and a team), we cannot change what we cannot see. Only when we see things differently, do new possibilities arise. To learn requires us to observe. Our capacity as leaders and teams to adapt and adjust and bring about new ways of thinking and doing are the most important competencies of our times.

To get the greatest value from this book, I invite you individually and collectively to be observers of the assessments, beliefs and perspectives you hold that may not serve you and that prevent you from seeing things differently. Reflect deeply on the questions posed throughout this book. Rather than rushing to an answer, stay in the question to allow more time for richer and deeper insights to emerge.

Learning is a social process that involves reflection and dialogue. Bring new insights to your team and work through them as a collective. Be open to what possibilities may arise.

Much of the power within teams lies in the disciplined application of what we hold as common sense about teams. This is explained further in each part of the book:

Part One: Why teams matter explores the distinctions between a group and a team and the attributes that make teams the predominant unit of organisational performance. We also explore the inherent paradoxes of teams—why high performing teams are so powerful but so rare. Finally, we discuss how teams have access to infinite potential once they unlock the collective capacity and capability to achieve the greatest things possible.

Part Two: How we team explores how pairing relationships and results distinguishes four types of teams: Combative, Competitive, Cohesive and Collaborative. Part Two introduces the 5 Disciplines of a High Performing Team that serve as the framework to enable teams to become high performing, collaborative and flourishing.

Part Three: What it takes to be an effective team elaborates on each of the 5 Disciplines: what they mean, why they are important and the results of 10 years of research on how teams perform against the 5 Disciplines. Finally, we explore what teams can do differently to embed the 5 Disciplines to become a high performing team.

Part Four: What is happening provides insight into the current reality for the many teams assessed through the 5 Disciplines and the possibilities for floundering teams to transition to flourish and operate at more than the sum of their parts for more of the time.

Part Five: Making it happen discusses how teams rise and fall based on the quality of their working relationships. Relationships happen in conversation. High performing teams distinguish themselves based on the quality of their conversations, in which nothing is 'undiscussable'.

Part Six: Team coaching is a learning journey that provides insight into what it takes for teams to transition to become collaborative, high performing teams—the design, the structure and the approach required to unlock the power in teams. The following table is an overview of my Team Coaching Program for High Performing Teams.

	LEARNING ACTIVITY	TIMELINE
1.	Discovery Phase (1:1 Discovery Conversations / Online Assessment / Debrief)	Conduct a 1:1 discovery conversation with each team member to assess the strengths and learning priorities of the team. Each team member will complete the *5 Disciplines of High Performing Teams Assessment* and results will be shared at the first team workshop. The discovery phase takes place 3–4 weeks before the first team workshop.
2.	Leadership Team Workshops (Offsite)	Five, 1-day workshops facilitated over 6–8 months.
3.	Peer Action-Learning Groups	Peer group coaching sessions to take place after each group workshop to support and enable team members to apply and embed their learning.
4.	Executive Coaching: Team Leader	Concurrent with the Team Coaching Program, the CEO or MD engages in a 1:1 executive coaching program for a 12-month period. An executive coaching program may also be extended to other leadership team members, dependent on their respective learning priorities.
5.	In-team Coaching: Leadership Team	Opportunity is provided for the facilitator to attend leadership team meetings to observe and provide feedback on the demonstrated application of the learning. This ensures the learning momentum is maintained and the return on the learning experience is realised.
6.	Return on Learning	One, 1-day workshop to be held 3–4 months after the Team Coaching Program to assess the return on the learning experience (R.O.L.E.). Opportunity will be provided to reassess the *5 Disciplines of High Performing Teams Assessment* and compare scores with the initial assessment results.

Part One
Why teams matter

Three paradoxes of a team

Most leaders know what distinguishes an effective team but their reality seldom represents the obvious. The obvious about teams is often mistaken to be easy.

Discipline is the antidote. Discipline does not make teaming easier but it does make it more possible. High performing teams have an uncompromising and relentless discipline in applying the essential elements that distinguish effective teams. Ignoring the essentials prevents teams from accessing their potential. For example, a shared purpose is essential to a team's success, yet many teams are unclear about their purpose. High performing teams are deliberate—their collective ways of being and doing are intentional. They accept there are no shortcuts to becoming a high performing team.

High performing teams happen by design. Good intentions and espoused commitment are no guarantee. Design is a consequence of discipline. High performing teams apply discipline. Teams do not become teams because they call themselves teams or because they have engaged in some 'team building' activity. Team building may help in getting to know people better, but discipline is essential to achieving as a team.

Likewise, having a detailed decision-making process map doesn't guarantee informed or better decisions. For teams to leverage diversity of thinking, they must gather a divergence of opinions so that greater understanding can emerge and from which more informed decisions can be made.

Much of what you will read in this book is common sense; however, it is not common practice. This is due to the inherent paradoxes in teams. In *The Paradox of Teamwork,* Gordon Rabey says,

> Teams ... have no identity, and recognition and reward remain focused on the individual. Yet the value and the power of the synergy of teamwork are unchallenged and ... [leaders] constantly seek to capture its benefits. Teams have the collective strength that will achieve targets and influence motivation and morale – but the ideas which stimulate their actions come from individuals, not necessarily their leaders. A team can incubate but it cannot initiate. Innovation begins when an idea and an individual meet...

As a team coach, I dedicate my time and energy to understanding and addressing the paradoxes in teams. In doing so, I have helped teams to unlock their power and access their collective capacity and capability to achieve the greatest things possible.

This book provides practical frameworks and approaches to understanding and overcoming the following three paradoxes:

1. Given that teams are the predominant unit of organisational performance, why are they preoccupied with tactical and operational issues and less focused on addressing the strategic and transformational imperatives?

2. Given that teams are so powerful, why is teamwork so rare? If teams create a sense of belonging and identity, why do many team members feel unsafe to speak their truth and discuss the undiscussables?

3. If teams have the potential to unlock their collective capacity and capability, why do they operate at less than the sum of their parts most of the time?

PARADOX ONE: TEAMS ARE THE PREDOMINANT UNIT OF ORGANISATIONAL PERFORMANCE

*'In every team, there is a group
but not every group is a team.'*
—John Kotter

Much is known and has been written about teams. There are many definitions of what constitutes a team. Common to all definitions, however, is the premise that accomplishing anything of value and meaning requires the coordination of action between at least two or more people. Teams matter because they exist to achieve what individuals cannot achieve by working independently of each other.

At the outset of a team coaching program, I often find that team members interchangeably call themselves the leadership 'group' and the leadership 'team'. Much can be different in a name. When invited to reflect on the differences between a group and a team, most do not see the distinctions. Groups and teams differ significantly and both have a role and place, albeit dissimilar.

For teams to be the predominant unit of organisational performance, it's important to understand the key distinctions between a group and a team.

A group is nothing more than a collection of individuals who independently contribute to a common objective, thus requiring low levels of integration and alignment. Working groups function well in certain contexts where complexity is low and the objectives are straightforward. However, they become less effective as the environment becomes more complex and the objectives become more challenging. When identifying and seizing synergies become a prerequisite for survival and long-term sustainability, a group must evolve into a team or it will drift into oblivion.

For example, committees, councils and review boards are not necessarily teams nor may they be required to operate as a team. More typically, they comprise individuals who only come together to inform each other of progress in their respective areas of responsibility and to share information that may be relevant to others.

Teams are the primary unit of performance in organisations. Only through teamwork can we combine different, complementary skills, knowledge and perspectives to identify and seize opportunities, overcome difficult obstacles and achieve challenging objectives.

Teams, unlike groups, operate from a unifying purpose, one that inspires the team members to a cause greater than themselves. Teams distinguish themselves by how they commit to engage and relate when together and apart, and above all they hold themselves and each other accountable to collective performance goals they know can be achieved only by working interdependently.

High performing teams develop a culture of their own. They visualise a shared future, motivate each other, learn from each other, resolve disputes and perform their jobs in ways that strengthen the overall system. In this way, they identify and seize synergy opportunities that realise an envisioned future.

High performing teams develop a culture based on humility, hard work, excellence and learning. The members become able to translate both their victories and their failures into inputs for continuous improvement. And each member develops unique, specialised skills that increase the team's inventory of competitive advantages. They periodically reinvent themselves and the way they work, thus quickly adapting to and generating new possibilities.

A summary of the key distinctions between a group and a team include:

A group of leaders	A leadership team
Deal best with complicated matters.	Deal best with complex situations.
Bring specialist knowledge to solve problems.	Bring collective experience, expertise and insight to understand the problem.
Follow existing processes and established practices.	Seek new ways and possibilities—take risks and experiment.
Focus on short-term results.	Focus on longer term benefits.
Impact is measured by progress and momentum.	Impact is brought about through transformational change.
Integrate performance and success.	Integrate performance and learning.
Individual accountability to domain specific KPIs.	Mutual accountability to collective goals.

PARADOX TWO: TEAMS ARE SO POWERFUL YET SO RARE

Several phenomena explain the power in teams. By way of context, Daniel Pink in his book, *Drive*, identifies three motivators that drive people to do their best at work: autonomy, mastery and purpose. Teams provide the structure and space to access and leverage these three motivators.

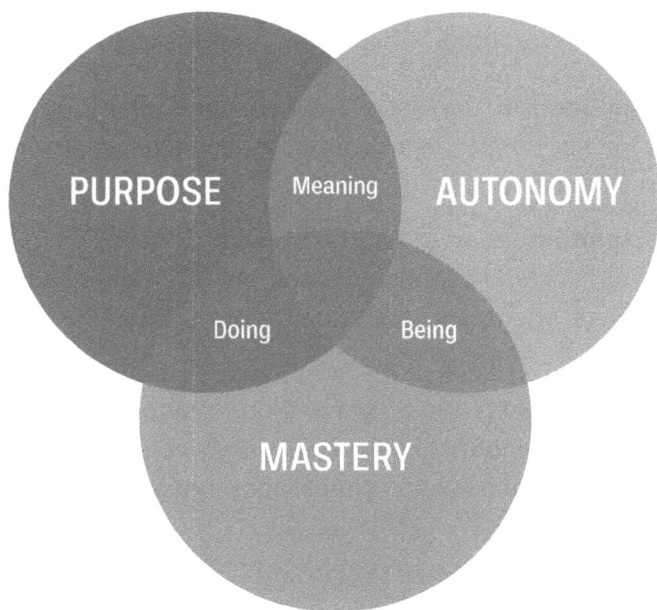

Let's explore each of the three motivators as the source of power in teams.

Purpose

Flourishing teams align to a common and shared purpose. Teams provide members with a sense of purpose, '... when members experience the work of their teams as being at least as important as their individual work,' says Ruth Wageman et al in their book, *Senior Leadership Teams*. 'Clarity of purpose makes the extraordinarily challenging and the consequential work of leadership teams feel possible. It orients the team in a way that allows it to pull together towards the same end, rather than pull – diligently if frustratingly – in different directions.'

Teams provide a unique opportunity to be part of something far greater than oneself. High performing teams provide members with a sense of purpose. This leaves them feeling:

- **Impactful:** The reason they exist and what they do has consequences, far beyond imagined, on all stakeholders.

- **Ignited:** Teams are at their best when their energy, passion and commitment are ignited by the continuous challenge to add real value to the organisation and its stakeholders.

- **Inspired:** Having a clear and common purpose inspires team members to identify why they need each other in order to achieve the critical challenges.

Autonomy

Teams exist to achieve the results that individuals working independently cannot reach. Teams have the autonomy to galvanise around performance challenges. Autonomy comes from the Greek word 'auto' meaning 'self' and 'nomos' meaning 'custom' or 'law'. High performing, autonomous teams are self-governing; they self-determine their purpose and the values to which they commit. Teams have the autonomy to determine the ways of working that enable them to best coordinate action. Most important, the power of a team is in the autonomy that exists to access collective wisdom to bring about new thinking and to create new ways of achieving the best outcomes.

As John Katzenbach and Douglas Smith shared in their book, *The Wisdom of Teams*, teams have the autonomy, '... in jointly developing clear goals and approaches ... are flexible and responsive to changing events ... adjust their approach to new information and challenges with greater speed, accuracy and effectiveness ...'

Mastery

Teams provide access to the wisdom inherent in the collective capacity and capability. Teams provide a depth of resourcefulness by bringing together complementary skills and experiences that exceed those of any individual on the team.

High performing teams distinguish themselves by the responsibility each member takes for their own and each other's learning. The openness to seek and offer feedback is fundamental to developing individual and collective mastery. Team members commit to learn with and from each other and collectively evolve and grow.

PARADOX THREE: POTENTIAL IN THE COLLECTIVE CAPACITY AND CAPABILITY

Teams have access to the collective capacity and capability, and the potential to achieve the greatest things possible. Imagine the teamwork required within NASA and between other stakeholders to successfully land the Perseverance Rover on Mars.

Michael Dell, founder and chairman of Dell Technologies, said, 'A culture of teamwork is an organisation's most competitive advantage ....'

While Dell's view is widely held to be true, reality would demonstrate that most teams operate at less than the sum of their parts most of the time. Part Two and Part Three provide further insight into why this may be so and what teams can do to access the power and potential in their collective capacity and capability.

Many executives attest that measuring teamwork is difficult. As Patrick Lencioni explains in *The Five Dysfunctions of a Team*, '[Teams] impact organisations in such comprehensive and invasive ways that it's virtually impossible to isolate it as a single variable. Many executives prefer solutions that are more easily measurable and verifiable, and so they look elsewhere for their competitive advantages.'

Having the brightest and most experienced team members with diverse skills and attributes does not necessarily guarantee access to the power and potential in a team. In his book, *Leading*

Teams, researcher Richard Hackman says, 'What teams need to thrive are certain enabling conditions.' In Part Three, we explore how the 5 Disciplines create 'enabling conditions' for teams to transition to become flourishing, high performing teams. These 'enabling conditions' include:

- A known mandate from the team's stakeholders.

- A clear and unifying purpose for why the team exists.

- Agreed and committed ways of working, and how team members relate and engage with one another and others.

- Common performance goals for which the team holds itself accountable and which can be achieved only by working interdependently.

- Commitment to learn with and from each other and evolve the collective wisdom.

Although the potential and power of teamwork cannot be denied, it can be difficult to measure and achieve. While teams may have access to infinite potential, it's not a given.

COMING UP IN PART TWO

Teams matter because they enable the performance outcomes that individuals working independently cannot. They provide members with a sense of belonging by identifying with a unifying purpose, the autonomy to access infinite possibilities, and the opportunity to learn and grow.

Accepting the importance of teams isn't a guarantee to experiencing the power in teams. Based on years of research and experience working with leadership teams, I will help you understand the reality of most teams and the possibilities to evolve, become and accomplish so much more than you believe possible.

Part Two
How we team

The ecosystem of a team

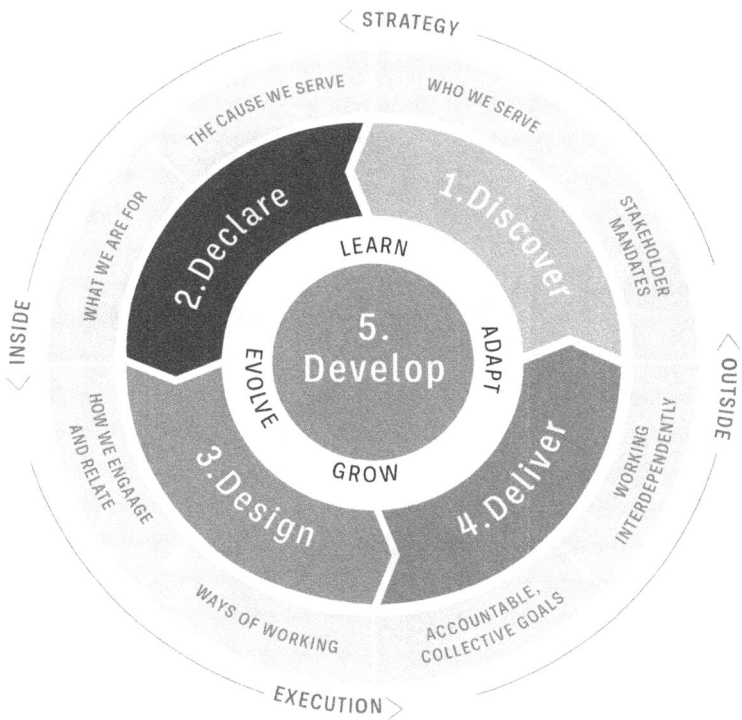

It's important to understand the context of how teams come into existence. All teams operate in an organisational context: an ecosystem of interdependent elements which, when in sync, combine to benefit all stakeholders. It's a broader system that brings relevance to why the team exists. There are four interdependent elements to a team's context:

1. Outside

Outside refers to the external stakeholders (those whom the team exists to serve). These stakeholder groups are varied and, more often than not, their interests, expectations and aspirations are assumed by team members.

What stakeholders require from the team (now and in the future) is fundamental in shaping and structuring the team's purpose, how team members commit to work together, and for what they hold themselves individually and collectively accountable to achieve. Where stakeholders' expectations are either assumed or misunderstood, teams flounder because members default to operating as a group of individuals working independently to achieve their own objectives.

High performing teams not only focus on their stakeholders' current challenges but anticipate their future requirements. As Peter Hawkins wrote in *Leadership Team Coaching*, 'Most teams work from "the past forward" trying to address current problems that have arisen from the past. More important is that teams focus "future-back" and focus on what their current and "not-yet" customers and stakeholders need different from them in the future.'

2. Strategy

Strategy represents the future that the team is commissioned to bring about. The organisational strategy aligns stakeholders' expectations of what success looks like with the team's understanding and commitment of what it will undertake to meet these expectations.

The organisational strategy defines the 'end in mind' that team members seek and strive to achieve. It represents the new possibilities and the unique value proposition that differentiates it from external competition.

Without a clear organisational strategy, teams risk turning their attention and action to what is most urgent rather than most important. Without a clear organisational strategy, matters of urgency and importance merge to mean and be the same.

2. Inside

Inside refers to the internal quality of the working relationships among the team members. Teams rise and fall based on the quality of their working relationships, and how they show up and relate when teaming together and apart. A team's 'way of being' together profoundly impacts its 'way of doing' together.

Teams who flourish do so because they invest time and effort in developing their interpersonal relationships. They recognise and accept that to get better results, they first need to develop better relationships together.

In high performing teams, better relationships precede better results.

4. Execution

Execution refers to how team members coordinate action by securing levels of cooperation and commitment to achieve what is most important. Execution at its essence is about the effectiveness of the requests team members make of others and the quality and trust they place in the commitments from others. But most importantly, execution is about team members accepting responsibility and holding themselves accountable to deliver on their promises and offers, and to acknowledge accomplishments by others once the conditions for success have been satisfactorily met.

Execution is about action: creating the desired future by getting things done.

TYPES OF TEAMS

A journey to becoming a high performing, effective team begins with an awareness of how the team shows up: How do team members experience being part of the team today? What is happening for team members when they 'team' together and apart? To what extent do team members feel energised by being together? Or do they feel, more often, that teaming together is a waste of time and effort? It is important for team members to reflect upon, share and discuss their answers to these questions.

To deny reality is a sure way to obstruct the possibility of change—awareness of reality is the starting point for any change. For floundering teams to transition to flourishing teams, they first have to acknowledge how their current reality may be hindering their accessibility to better ways of being and ways of doing. Only then is it possible to adopt a different mindset and belief system that enables the team to adapt behaviours and achieve what is only possible by working more collaboratively.

I want to share two perspectives about our human existence that can make it difficult for teams to access their potentiality.

Breakdowns

As humans (individuals, teams, groups or communities) we are continually dealing with breakdowns: the unanticipated interruptions and interferences to our habitual flow of living, working and being. Most of the time we default to reacting and unconsciously dealing with these breakdowns based on our accumulative experience and knowledge of what has worked for us in the past. For example, along my habitual home-to-work travelling route, I am confronted by a road closure caused by a burst water main. Having been marshalled to take an alternative route, I am concerned that I will be late for my meeting and be an inconvenience to my client. Breakdown! Once I collect my thoughts and consider my options, I take action. I notify the client of my circumstances and manage their expectations around a revised meeting start time. Problem solved.

Breakdowns are an inevitable aspect of human existence: we live and lead in uncertainty. We know for certain that Wednesday comes after Tuesday but we don't know for certain what those days will bring. Breakdowns call upon teams to learn, adapt and adjust to how they deal with increasing levels of uncertainty and complexity synonymous with life as we know it today.

We live and work in increasingly complex, changing and uncertain times. Our existing knowledge, experience and skills may not be enough to deal with unprecedented breakdowns. Point in case is COVID-19. Pandemics are 'collective breakdowns' that affect people all over the world. Collective breakdowns— as we have experienced—can have catastrophic consequences on personal and professional lives and livelihoods.

Life's breakdowns call on us individually and collectively to adapt and adjust to different ways of being and to new ways of doing. While breakdowns are more commonly experienced as negative, they *can* also be positive. For example, winning a significant tender to deliver the biggest piece of work ever undertaken causes a positive breakdown.

A team's ability to shift to become a flourishing, high performing team is largely dependent upon the team's ability to acknowledge and effectively deal with individual *and* collective breakdowns.

> *'When nothing is sure,*
> *everything is possible.'*
> —Margaret Drabble

Concerns

As humans, we are never not concerned. We are continually listening, thinking, speaking and acting from what is important to us about what isn't going to plan. For example, I may be concerned about a deteriorating relationship with a colleague. Increasingly, I find it harder to trust them because they have let me down on a few occasions and I have heard, from others, various derogatory comments they have made about me. Each time I find myself in their presence, my listening, thinking, speaking and acting comes from a concern I hold about their untrustworthiness.

To unlock a team's power and access its collective capacity and capability, each team member must acknowledge and legitimise their own and each other's concerns—their 'known spoken' and their 'known unspoken' concerns. By 'known spoken' concerns, I mean matters of importance, which team members feel confident and comfortable to call out, discuss and address among themselves in a safe and supported environment. But more importantly, team members need to acknowledge their 'known unspoken' concerns. These concerns are often avoided or denied because of the perceived consequences of attempting to discuss the undiscussable.

A characteristic of competitive teams is they operate in an environment where more concerns are unspoken rather than spoken. Collaborative teams accept the normality of uncertainty and deal with what is important. A hallmark of a collaborative, high performing team is there are no unspoken concerns. A high performing team expresses rather than suppresses its concerns. It's suppressing rather than expressing our concerns that gives rise to dysfunctional interpersonal relationships.

A team's capacity to become high performing is dependent upon the team members' ability to deal with their own and each other's concerns. To hold one's own and others' concerns with respect, dignity and legitimacy is what distinguishes high performing, effective teams. (I will elaborate more about concerns and the role they play in teams in a subsequent chapter.)

TEAM VALUE MODEL

	STYLE	STATE	IMPACT	
Creative	Collaborative	Flourishing	●	High impact
Creative	Cohesive	Functioning	◑	High impact
Reactive	Competitive	Floundering	◐	Low impact
Reactive	Combative	Failing	◔	Low impact

Figure 1: Team Value Model

Teams differ based on their orientation towards operating from their 'reactive tendencies' or their 'creative potential'. Let's explore the two reactive and creative team types.

Reactive teams

When faced with unanticipated interruptions and interferences, reactive teams are seduced into an automatic response. Unconscious patterns of thinking and behavioural repertoires dominate and prevent teams from accessing new possibilities and finding new ways of dealing with the reality of uncertainty and change. They feel and get stuck. Reactive teams have low impact. They maintain and defend the status quo. They are governed by how things have always been done.

Reactive teams feel unsafe to
challenge established ways.

Team members engage in 'cordial hypocrisy'. They feel unsafe to speak their truth or to disagree with the prevailing views and decisions. Experience has taught them there's more often a price to be paid for disagreeing or offering differing perspectives. Reactive teams hold a space of destructive content; they shroud themselves in a veil of harmony and direct their energy to avoid conflict and disagreement.

Combative teams

Combative team members show up with self-centred, egotistical behaviours, and their motives and ideals are driven by self-preservation and benefit. Combative teams are characterised by high levels of dysfunctional relationships and patterns of behaviour. High levels of distrust, disregard and disrespect exist. Each member is in it for themselves: one's gain is another's loss. The predominant mood is one of resentment where team members undermine each other and actively hinder each member's ability to succeed. Revenge is more often the primary motive in combative teams.

The inevitable consequence of a
combative team is failure.

I was engaged to help the leadership team of a technology start-up to work more effectively. The team comprised three entrepreneurs who believed their collective experience, skillset and attributes could be leveraged to bring new offerings to market. However, this once harmonious group soon devolved into a combative team. From early in our engagement, it was apparent that no one was prepared to acknowledge the others' strengths and expertise. Each felt their ideas and perspectives were more credible and hence more worthy of consideration. There was no space to learn from their differences—each only defended their own qualities. The inevitable consequence was failure and eventual bankruptcy.

Competitive teams

An internal win-lose mindset predominates competitive teams. Team members exert their power over each other not with each other. Internal competition is more consuming than external competition. Much of the team members' time, energy and actions are directed toward competing for their share in voice, value and vanity. Dominant team members hog meetings and challenge others as egos come into play. To win means to ensure one's opinion prevails and one's own results matter the most. During conversations, more reference is made to 'me, my and I' rather than 'you, us and our'.

Most of the team's effort and energy is directed at reacting to the issues in front of it: the day-to-day operational and tactical issues. Little consideration and time are spent coordinating thinking, scanning the environment or proactively dealing with important or strategic considerations.

Individual members exert control by focusing on what they know, understand and do best. They operate in silos and rarely contribute ideas and insights outside of their domain of responsibility and capability for fear of being accused of interfering and undermining.

Competitive teams feel unsafe. Rather than dealing with matters in an open and transparent manner, they default to being passively aggressive, which results in more being unspoken than spoken.

Team members tend to not advocate their true feelings and perspectives nor do they inquire into others'. Most of their time is spent assuming and assessing what others think and feel, and less is known about what they actually think and feel. Competitive teams operate in survival mode: they are putting out fires rather than working out how to prevent them.

> Competitive teams operate at less than the sum of their parts, and find it difficult to mobilise the collective capacity and capabilities inherent in the team.

Competitive teams flounder. They are unable to mobilise the collective capacity and capabilities inherent in the team.

Creative teams

Creative teams access their collective capacity and capability to identify, explore and experiment with new and different ways. They create a motivational environment that extends far beyond the team members. They give cause for others to follow them. They inspire belief in what is possible, and they mobilise others to see and commit to new possibilities. They instil a level of confidence in others that makes it safe and possible to experiment, take risks and learn from their mistakes. Creative teams have high impact.

> Creative teams sustain an organisation's most
> competitive advantage—a culture of teamwork.

Creative teams do not happen by accident; they happen by design. The intentionality of creative teams differentiates them. Creative teams lean into constructive discontent; they challenge how things are done with the intention of finding better ways of delivering better results. Creative teams instil a culture of teamwork that cascades throughout the organisation. They secure the most sustainable competitive advantage: a culture of teamwork. A culture of teamwork is the only thing competitors cannot copy.

Cohesive teams

Cohesive teams bring stability by reacting to what must be dealt with and by accessing the collective capacity, capability and commitment needed to create a more desired future. Cohesive teams feel 'functional'. Team members consistently show up with a win-win mindset. Their attention, energy and activity are directed towards aligned objectives. Team members value and appreciate the quality of their working relationships. They share greater levels of mutual trust and hold each other's differing perspectives with respect rather than judgement.

Cohesive teams bring a balance of requisite and diverse skills, and experience and knowledge. They more consistently operate at the sum of their parts but rarely greater than the sum of their parts. A cohesive team is typically regarded highly by stakeholders (a 'safe set of hands') and can be relied upon to get the job done.

Functional teams arise when team members feel
safe to express and not suppress their truth.

Because of the 'functional' nature of cohesive teams, some members can be blind to their potential liabilities. There are three 'enemies' to which cohesive teams need to be alert:

1. Default to consensus

Functional teams lean towards agreement rather than seeking out differences. They look for commonality of thinking and perspectives rather than exploring diversity of thinking. They tend to rely on the tried and tested ways of doing things as opposed to considering alternate and potentially better ways. They seek to achieve consensus favoured by the majority. This only serves teams when dealing with common problems with known and tested solutions.

Consensus may blind functional teams from exploring new possibilities when faced with solving complex issues.

2. The shroud of harmony

This enemy prevails when functional teams choose agreement over disagreement. Because they value their working relationships, conflict can be perceived as undermining and damaging to relationships. When conflict is believed to be bad and wrong, the shroud of harmony blows over. Keeping the peace is valued over constructive conflict because it feels uncomfortable.

There is nothing inherently wrong with seeking and being in harmony; however, harmony can have a dark side when it is used as a means of avoiding difficult conversations. Functional teams are less comfortable being uncomfortable.

3. Engage in 'cordial hypocrisy'

Team members who seek and value agreement and avoid the risk of conflict engage in 'cordial hypocrisy'. When difficult situations arise—like having courageous conversations—team members withhold speaking their truth and only say what they believe others want to hear.

Dysfunctional relationships arise when team members suppress rather than express their truth.

Collaborative teams

Collaborative teams differentiate themselves by coming together, staying together and achieving together (as 'one'). Team members share a 'win for all' mindset when teaming together and apart. A collaborative team operates from a unifying purpose: members are unified in serving a cause greater than themselves; they commit to adopting a common approach to how they engage when together and apart; and, above all, they hold themselves and each other accountable to collective performance goals they can only achieve by working interdependently.

They develop a culture of their own. They visualise a shared future: they motivate each other, learn from each other, resolve disputes and perform their roles in ways that strengthen the overall system. In this way, they identify and seize synergic opportunities.

Collaborative teams develop a culture based
on humility, courage, excellence and learning.

They translate their victories and failures into learning and
continuous improvement. Each member develops unique,
specialised skills that increase the team's inventory of
competitive advantages. They reinvent themselves and the
way they work, thus quickly adapting to and generating new
possibilities.

Collaborative teams enable organisations to secure their most
competitive advantage: a culture of teamwork. They flourish in
how they bring about new possibilities, and they have a lasting
positive impact on all their stakeholders. They operate at more
than the sum of their parts for more of the time.

Collaborative teams flourish by accessing their collective
capacity and capability. Collaborative teams distinguish
themselves by their uncompromising collective commitment to
embed the 5 Disciplines unique to high performing teams.

COMING UP IN PART THREE

Teams who accept the interdependence between the four elements of a team's ecosystem open themselves to embody the 5 Disciplines that distinguish high performing teams. In Part Three, I turn our attention to each discipline: what it means, what it involves and the possibilities it presents for your team.

The single most important distinction between a *functional* and a *flourishing* team is the unconditional commitment team members make to embed the 5 Disciplines into their ways of being and doing together. Flourishing teams can't 'not team' from these 5 Disciplines.

Part Three

What it takes to be an effective team

The 5 Disciplines of a team

Having explored the different types of teams, you now have a point of reference from which to commence your journey to becoming a flourishing, high performing team. But what does it actually take to become part of a high performing team?

> Effective teams outperform
> effective leaders, every time.

The 5 Disciplines represent common sense and here we will learn how to transition them into common practice. Each discipline signifies what is needed to create an environment where team members are invested in each other's success, and where they learn from each other as they work interdependently to identify and achieve the team's objectives.

The art of discipline has been discussed for thousands of years and has its origins from the Ancient Greek philosophy of 'sophrosyne', which means an 'ideal of excellent character and soundness of mind that leads to moderation, self-control and balance'. It is through discipline that team members choose and then persevere with actions, thoughts and behaviours that lead to improvement and success. Discipline gives team members the power and inner strength to overcome the unanticipated interruptions and interferences that form the normality of the uncertainty that is life.

DISCOVER	1.	The team has a clear commission and mandate from its stakeholders and those it reports to.
	2.	The team relates well to all its key stakeholders with the team members representing the whole team.
	3.	The team has been selected to have the complementary skills to achieve its mandate.
DECLARE	4.	Team members understand, can articulate and are committed to the team's purpose.
	5.	Team members know and consistently uphold the team's values.
DESIGN	6.	The team behaviours and shared 'ways of working' have been identified and are consistently upheld.
	7.	The team members secure cooperation and commitment from each other.
	8.	Team members are mutually accountable for their own areas of responsibility and the team's collective goals.
	9.	All team members are engaged and involved, and the team makes good use of its diversity.
DELIVER	10.	The team has clear collective performance goals which can be achieved only by working interdependently.
	11.	Achieving the team's goals is recognised and rewarded above achieving individual goals.
	12.	The outcomes achieved are better than any individual could arrive at by themselves.
	13.	Team members leave meetings feeling more focused, supported, and energised.
	14.	The team scans its stakeholders' environment and constantly attends to changing needs and perceptions.
	15.	Team members engage employees at all levels as transformational leaders.

DEVELOP	16. Team members are open to receiving and giving feedback to each other on their performance and behaviours.
	17. Team members support each other and are committed to each other's ongoing learning and development.
	18. Team members keep challenging themselves and others to keep developing and adding greater value

'A team operating without a mandate risks getting better and better at doing what is not wanted by their stakeholders.'

—Peter Hawkins

To be a collaborative, high performing team, and to be sustainably effective and value-creating, it is essential to have each of the disciplines. It's important to appreciate the consequences of each discipline being compromised:

1. If the Discipline to Discover is ignored, teams operate in a vacuum of understanding of their stakeholders' expectations and invest time and energy delivering what is not wanted from their stakeholders.

2. If the Discipline to Declare is ignored, team members don't share a common understanding of the team's purpose and reason for existence. This makes it difficult to secure collective ownership of the team's direction and focus.

3. If the Discipline to Design is ignored, it will result in wasted energy and effort from a lack of understanding and commitment to agreed ways of working and an inability to secure the levels of cooperation and commitment required to achieve collective goals.

4. If the Discipline to Deliver is ignored, team members direct their individual attention and activity to tasks they feel most confident in and have the greatest control over rather than looking to leverage the collective synergies required to achieve the team's performance goals.

5. If the Discipline to Develop is ignored, team members are less open to learning with and from one another, therefore missing the opportunity to learn from their successes and mistakes. They do not harness the collective wisdom and capacity needed to succeed.

DISCIPLINE #1: DISCOVER OUR MANDATE

The team's mandate

Mandates are sought and known, not assumed. As Hawkins shared, 'For a team to be successful, it needs a clear commission from those who bring it into existence.' The mandate is more than what the team is expected to accomplish. It seeks to clarify:

1. What stakeholders appreciate about the team and what they recognise as its differentiating qualities.

2. How stakeholders want teams to deliver value and how the leadership can be more effective.

3. What stakeholders think about their relationship with the team and how it can be improved.

The team's mandate sets the scope and boundaries within which it is expected to operate. It is the terms of reference with which the stakeholders commission the team. The mandate brings needed clarity to the following:

1. What can this team achieve that no other group of individuals can?

2. What is the scope and range of topics upon which the team will focus?

3. How will we measure success of the work the team delivers?

When I asked a senior leadership team of a division that serviced a large and significant government agency about their stakeholders' mandate, I was met with blank faces rather than certain responses.

Over the years of working with teams, I've come to realise that most teams *assume* rather than *know* their stakeholders' mandate. Often, teams I've worked with feel it's their responsibility to set and not seek the mandate. Teams exist to serve the mandate stakeholders commission the team to deliver upon. Mandates are to be known and not assumed. In the absence of an understood mandate (one the team owns and commits to deliver upon), the team defaults to service its own interests.

Teams are often faced with having to satisfy many and varied stakeholder mandates, some of which may be in conflict. Take, for example, the finance team of a large publicly listed organisation who must ensure that the interests and mandate of team members, clients, local and foreign government regulatory bodies, suppliers, investors and individual shareholders, communities, and the board and executive team are understood and delivered upon.

I liken a team's mandate to the baton in a relay team—passed between runners and carried over the line. The baton is a physical representation of the mandate a team has been commissioned to 'get across the line'. This is what stakeholders expect the team to deliver.

The diagram below illustrates what constitutes a team's mandate and what it should engage with its stakeholders about.

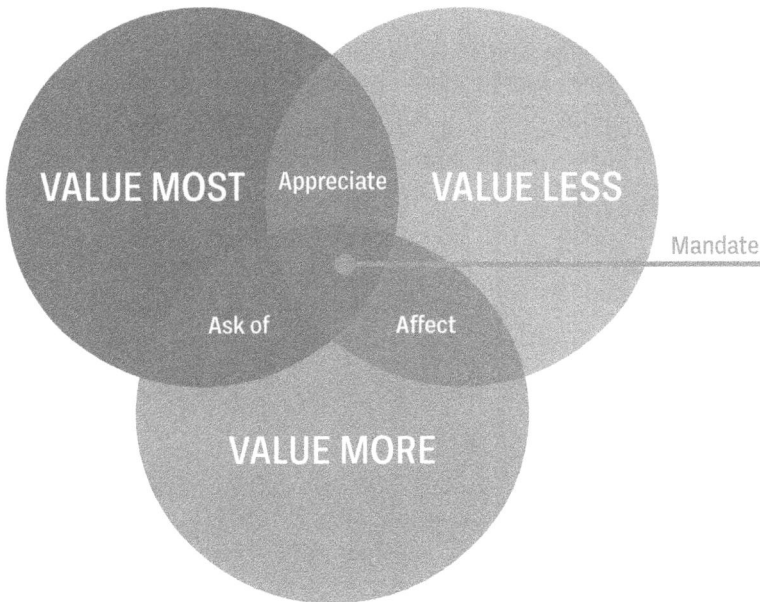

First, it is important the team understands and appreciates what their stakeholders value most about it. By this, I mean the attributes and characteristics of the team that give stakeholders the confidence and conviction that the team is best positioned to succeed. It's important that the team continuously plays to and leverages what stakeholders value most about it.

Second, what do stakeholders value less about the team? These are the concerns stakeholders believe may affect the team's ability to deliver to their expectations and what they find difficult in their relationship with the team. In addition, it's those areas of focus and expectations the team are not consistently delivering upon or the challenges the team may not be anticipating they would have to deal with and overcome.

Third, and possibly most important, is what stakeholders expect more of (or something different) from the team. What are stakeholders looking to the team to step up to? What may have changed in how stakeholders assess the team's success and value add? What may stakeholders expect of the team who has neither the capacity nor capability to deliver?

The answers to these questions require regular and proactive engagement with stakeholder groups. High performing teams take responsibility to continuously review and revise the mandate and confirm what their stakeholders expect and value from the team.

Teams exist to serve their stakeholders. Therefore, it's the stakeholders who commission the team with its mandate. The mandate states that which the team is looked upon to represent and deliver.

DISCIPLINE #2: DECLARE OUR PURPOSE

"If we have our own 'why' of life we shall get along with almost any 'how'."
—Friedrich Nietzsche

As German poet and playwright Johann Wolfgang von Goethe once said, 'One must be something in order to do something.' A team's purpose represents its reason for being. The purpose creates the team; the team does not create the purpose. It speaks to why the team exists, not what the team does. A team's purpose serves as the unifying reason why the team starts together, stays together and strives for a cause greater than itself.

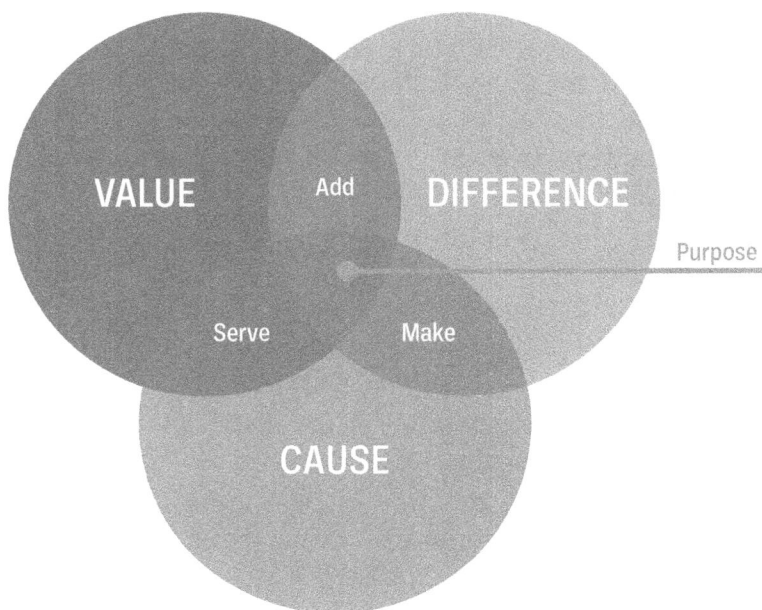

VALUE Add DIFFERENCE

Purpose

Serve Make

CAUSE

The team's purpose is captured in its collective responses to these questions:

1. What value does the team add and what difference does it make to those who follow?

2. What cause, greater than itself, does the team serve?

3. For what sake has the team come into being?

The team's purpose

There are two important days for any team: the day it is formed and the day it discovers its purpose. Purpose matters. Purpose energises.

Nikos Mourkogiannis, author of *Purpose*, says, 'Purpose makes work meaningful and integrates it into our lives; it enables us to feel proud in what we do and liberates us to do better.' As humans, we are intrinsically driven to find meaning in what we do. We are meaning-making machines and as such we are more than human beings—we are human becomings, always leaning into and creating new futures. Our collective pursuit to discover new and better ways to deliver greater value provides us with a sense of fulfilment and achievement.

As Peter Hawkins reminds us, '... it is the purpose that creates the team, not the team that creates the purpose. The purpose precedes the team. If there was not a purpose to respond to or fulfil, there would be no need for a team.' The value in what teams do is a reflection of their purpose. A floundering competitive team focuses on *what* it does while a flourishing collaborative team focuses on *why* it does it. Teams exist to accomplish something collectively that they could not accomplish separately. To unlock the power in a team, members must align to a unifying and common purpose. A purpose is the source of a team's energy. Any loss of energy in a team is caused by a lessening of its purpose.

Ruth Wageman offers the following perspective on purpose: '... the team's purpose is not merely the sum of the individual member's contribution, nor is it the purpose of the organisation. The team's purpose answers the question, what is the team for that no other entity in the organisation could accomplish?'

More often than not, when I ask team members to clarify their team's purpose, they default to explaining what they do and not why they do it. I asked a senior leadership team in the financial services sector to share what it believed to be its team's purpose. Without hesitation, the majority declared its purpose was to 'deliver a profit to the shareholders'. After some discussion, it was recognised that to deliver a profit was a consequence of what it did and not why it was created.

Following a facilitated process (details of which I will explain later in the chapter), the team agreed that its purpose as the senior leadership team was:

To serve its colleagues, clients, customers and communities.

The unifying clarity of its purpose had a significant impact on how team members come together and achieve together. Most significant of all, an agreed purpose enabled the team to align and agree on collective performance goals.

> Clarity of purpose is the starting point of greatness. It enables access to the collective capacity and capability inherent in teams.

There is no question that every company has to achieve a profit to survive, grow and prosper. But this does not mean the leadership teams exist to maximise profits. They exist to create an environment in which everyone finds meaning and where they are energised by contributing to something greater than themselves. When this occurs, a sustainable profitable outcome is more likely.

To sustain a team's focus and energy to accomplish what is most important, members need to understand why the team was created.

Telltale signs of a team's misaligned purpose

Some of the more common indicators of a misaligned understanding of a team's purpose include:

1. Certain reputational challenges that stakeholders keep coming back to. For example, where employees believe the leadership team members do not consistently 'walk their talk', or where the customer Net Promoter Scores (NPS) keep decreasing or investors keep divesting.

2. Where the working relationships between team members are not as effective as they need to be. This is often due to a lack of trust between team members. So, more is unspoken than spoken among team members and concerns remain unresolved, which contributes to the further deterioration of their working relationships.

3. When energy and effort are placed in achieving individual objectives rather than in the team's collective performance goals. In such instances, team members

focus on what they are most confident in and feel they have more control over—their silo.

4. Mistrust and focusing on individual objectives, which make it challenging to secure the levels of commitment and cooperation from each other to work more interdependently to achieve collective objectives.

5. Resistance to change. When a team looks for reasons and excuses for why change is less likely to yield the desired outcome, the team becomes stuck. Members are not open to learning with and from one another. This is the most telling sign of a team's misaligned purpose.

Take the opportunity to reflect on the teams you lead and ask yourself to what extent are one or more of these indicators currently playing out. Then commit to addressing them.

What it takes to be purposeful

Team members are not loyal to a 'profit target'; they are loyal to the team's values and to the greater cause central to the team's existence.

To help identify a unifying and common team purpose, reflect and share thought on the following:

1. What value does the team add to those it serves?

This question is intended to bring focus to what the stakeholders look to the team to deliver and achieve.

2. What difference does the team make to those who follow?

This question seeks to distinguish the team from those less able to secure followers. What unique qualities does the team have that encourages others to trust, respect and follow it?

3. What cause does the team serve greater than itself?

This is the essence of the team's existence. It addresses what the team stands for and the cause the team serves that is greater than the needs of the individuals.

The difference a purpose can make

I was working with the regional senior leadership team of a global medical technology company. The team unanimously felt it lacked a common purpose and was not operating to its full potential. It felt stuck in patterns of behaviours that undermined its ability to access and leverage its collective capacity. Its lack of common purpose manifested in several undesirable ways:

1. The team backtracked on decisions and overthought things because of a lack of trust in each other's judgement.

2. Important decisions were made in isolation, which made it difficult to secure commitment and coordinate action.

3. Team members looked to blame one another when things did not go as planned. They avoided taking responsibility for delivering outcomes outside of their own areas of responsibility.

4. Team meetings were unproductive, draining and frustrating. Progress wasn't enabled.

As part of the team coaching process, I asked each member to review the questions on finding their team purpose (see above: 'What it takes to be purposeful'). Then they were placed in small groups to share their insights before coming together to share the trends and patterns that emerged. The smaller group discussions served to create a safer space to share their thinking thus enabling a richer and more inclusive conversation as a team.

To enable the team to craft a common purpose, each team member was invited to select one out of 250 images that they felt most strongly represented what they believed to be the team's purpose. Using a visual metaphor reinforces the power of imagery to elicit more effective, creative and insightful dialogue. Most importantly, using a visual metaphor legitimises the diversity of perspectives to be accessed to secure team members' buy-in and commitment.

Following this exercise, the collective energy enabled the team to agree on its purpose:

We change lives for the better.

As the managing director reflected, 'Aligning ourselves to a common purpose and committing to agreed ways of working has enabled us, as the leadership team, to achieve together what we could not have working independently of each other.'

Nine months after the leadership team identified its purpose, we regrouped to reflect on the impact it felt its purpose had on how it now 'teamed better together'. Here is some of what was shared:

- The greatest impact came from sharing stories with staff, customers and consultants about how they 'lived' their purpose. Sharing stories about how people's lives had changed as a result of the treatment and how more self-assured and confident they felt brought greater happiness.

- Team members felt they had built greater levels of trust and respect among themselves. This enabled them to better align and coordinate action to achieve their common goals. Over the same period they achieved a compound annual growth rate (CAGR) of 34%.

- The team ensured its purpose served as the 'clear thread through everything we do'. It served to inspire, energise, align and, above all, unite the team to a common cause.

DISCIPLINE #3: DESIGN OUR CULTURE

High performing teams commit to a greater understanding of each other's perspectives so they can make more informed decisions and take wiser action. High performing teams commit to creating a distinguishing culture. The team's culture is the agreed ways of being that best serve the team in how team members engage and relate when teaming together and apart.

High performing teams design a way of being that is built upon mutual respect and trust, and where team members feel safe and supported to speak their truth. The team's culture manifests through conversation: what team members think, say and do that enables them to secure others' cooperation and commitment to get done what is most important.

The team's culture is represented by the team's collective responses to these questions:

1. How will we engage and relate with each other when teaming together and apart?

2. What do we want others to think and feel after each engagement with our team?

3. What ways of working do we commit to upholding when teaming together and apart?

The team's culture

One of the biggest downfalls of organisations today is not doing things consistently and effectively. Increasingly, balls are dropped, deadlines are missed, priorities are constantly changed, and projects run over time and budget. Furthermore, change is unsatisfactorily managed.

Teams are the primary unit of performance in organisations. Teams are about getting things done by interacting with others to ensure work flows smoothly and is completed satisfactorily. For work to flow smoothly, team members must coordinate action through securing one another's cooperation and commitment.

Relationships are the lifeblood of effective teamwork. Team members continuously interact with one another through conversation. Their conversational proficiency determines how well the strategies, plans, policies, systems and processes are implemented to achieve the desired results.

Diverging and conflicting perspectives are more prevalent in teams and organisations than ever before. Despite being more connected, having access to more information and working longer hours, we are increasingly overwhelmed by the demands on our time and attention. Discernment is reduced and the quality of decision-making and problem-solving is compromised. Working relationships deteriorate and people remain stuck in recurring patterns of behaviour that produce suboptimal results.

Why are high performing teams still so rare given that they are so powerful?

This question has preoccupied my thinking and work for the past 10 years. In this chapter, we explore the role that interpersonal relationships play in enabling teams to evolve and transform into collaborative, high performing teams where great outcomes are possible. When referencing effective relationships, it's important to understand that I am not talking about friendships. Friendships are a by-product of the respect, trust and mutual appreciation shared between others. The central premise is that the quality of working relationships is a key variable in high performing teams. While organisational excellence involves a range of dimensions to do with systems, processes and structures, the central pivot to sustainable organisational success is the quality of the team members working relationships.

> Improved relationships lead to improved results.

The Discipline to Design addresses how teams design their ways of working that ensure team members engage and relate so they can best coordinate and cooperate to achieve what only teams can. Effective working relationships are not the end; rather they ensure team members secure greater levels of cooperation and commitment to coordinate action to achieve what is most important. Quality relationships precede quality results.

Given that teams are the predominant unit of organisational performance, nothing of value and meaning can be created without teaming. It therefore follows that a culture of teamwork is the most sustainable competitive advantage any organisation can secure over their competitors.

Teams, besides being the predominant unit of organisational performance, provide members with a sense of belonging and identity. As social and relational beings, our existence depends upon our ability to engage and relate with others who believe what we believe. Teams are our tribes. Never has this been more evident than during the COVID-19 lockdowns where teams served as the medium for connection, care and coordination. 2020 and 2021 have proved that organisations with a strong culture of teamwork can best adapt and adjust to deal with unprecedented levels of uncertainty and change. Teamwork does not necessarily make things easier but it makes more things possible. Teamwork is like a marriage: take it for granted and it's likely to fall apart.

The dimensions of effective relationships

Teams who commit to establishing and maintaining effective working relationships create the possibility to operate at more than the sum of their parts and achieve extraordinary results. The better the relationships, the better the results.

How team members show up is revealed in their way of being and how they assess and perceive the world. The world as we experience it is not as it is; it is as we are. For example, if a particular team member feels unsafe to speak their truth or challenge the predominant view, their way of being will likely elicit a level of fear and anxiety that leads them to choose silence over sharing.

Our way of being profoundly affects our way of doing. How we perceive any event or situation profoundly affects how we choose to react or deal with the situation. Based on the modified and expanded model originally presented by Gloria Kelly (a pre-eminent sociologist), there are eight dimensions to an effective working relationship. There are five areas that relate to our relational way of being (how we perceive the world) and three that relate to our relational way of doing (how we interact with the world).

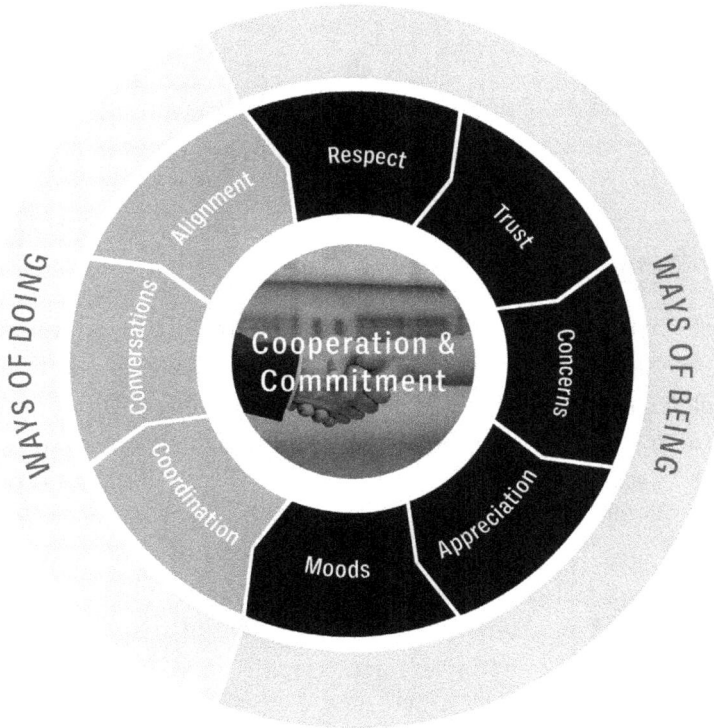

Before we can work with these dimensions, we must ensure a common and consistent understanding of what each dimension means and how each one contributes to building effective working relationships. In sharing these definitions, I acknowledge the work and contribution of Alan Sieler, founder of the Newfield Institute.

The five dimensions relevant to our 'way of being' as a team

1. Respect

Respect is holding others in acceptance and legitimacy. Acceptance does not mean having to agree with others' views; it means holding others' views, perspectives and opinions with dignity and legitimacy despite how similar or different they may be to your own or how strongly you may feel about a particular viewpoint.

Holding others with respect means committing to understanding rather than judging their views. Only when we show up to and look to 'the legitimate other' can we genuinely respect others as fellow humans in their similarities and differences to us.

Alan Sieler reminds us that, 'There can be a tendency for us to not only be dismissive of others' views but also of them as people (i.e. not hold them as being a legitimate human being) when we label them wrong or negatively in response to the views and opinions they are expressing.'

At its core, respect is about legitimising others with dignity. The greatest gift one can give to another is to leave them feeling respected by you.

2. Trust

As Patrick Lencioni says, 'Trust lies at the heart of a collaborative team. Without it, teamwork is all but impossible.'

Research by Edelman shows that the level of trust in societal institutions, particularly business, government and media, has declined over the past decade and shows no signs of improving.

The quintessence of an effective relationship is the level of trust the parties have in one another. So, what do we mean when we say we trust someone? Based on the Trust Equation developed by David Maister, author of *The Trusted Advisor*, trust is composed of four interdependent elements, each of which needs to be adequately demonstrated to earn others' trust:

a. **Credibility** refers to the extent to which one perceives the other to have the technical skills, knowledge and expertise to do what is expected of them. However, credibility isn't just about content expertise, it is also about the other's 'presence'—the extent to which we assess how others look, act, react and talk about their content. Perception is reality.

b. **Reliability** refers to the extent to which one will likely do what they commit to. Reliability is the one component of the trust equation with an explicit action orientation. It links words and deeds, intention and action. This action orientation distinguishes reliability from credibility. A promise made is a promise kept. Reliability in a rational sense is the repeated experience of links between promises and action. We judge someone's reliability with due dates and quality levels—on time and on spec.

c. **Intimacy** refers to the emotional intimacy shared as opposed to the personal closeness. Not that one must divulge what is personal and private but to be vulnerable about sharing one's feelings and thoughts—

the preparedness to speak our truth while holding the other with respect, dignity and legitimacy. Intimacy is most often more scarce compared to credibility and reliability. People trust those with whom they will talk about difficult agendas and those who demonstrate that they care.

d. **Self-orientation** refers to the extent to which others experience us placing their interests above our own. This does not necessarily mean it has to be at the expense of one's own interests but to focus more on what is of greatest value and benefit to the other. There is no greater source of distrust than those who appear to be more interested in themselves than in trying to be of service to others.

3. Concerns

As humans, we live 'in concern'. We are always thinking, listening, speaking and acting from what is important to us. We are continuously addressing what we care most about. We are never not 'in concern'. To build an effective relationship, we must understand and appreciate what is important to others. What we care about is at the heart of our being. Continue to ask yourself what is important to you and to the other party in this relationship, and how well is this (are these) being addressed.

4. Appreciation

It is important to feel valued and appreciated for your work efforts and for who you are. It is a fundamental concern, as a human, to feel recognised, acknowledged, valued and appreciated. It's important to distinguish between recognition and appreciation, however. While it could be argued that they are different sides of the same coin, they differ. We typically recognise others for what they have achieved or accomplished. We typically apply the Recognition Award for having achieved a level or measure of performance. We recognise others for what has happened.

Conversely, to show appreciation for others is more often referring to what we appreciate about who they are and what they mean to us. We appreciate others' insights and advice, their 'pats on the back' and the 'thank-you' praise. We appreciate knowing that we can turn to them in times of need.

It is equally important to recognise others for what they have accomplished and to appreciate them for who they are.

5. Moods

Biologically, we are inescapably emotional beings. We are never not 'in mood'. Everything we say or do is because of the mood we're in. Moods are a predisposition for action. It is difficult to be influenced by someone who irritates or annoys you. You may say, 'I'm interested to know what you think about my idea'; however, the little voice in your head is screaming, *I couldn't give a damn what they think. I'm going ahead regardless.*

To build effective working relationships, it is essential to be an observer of one's moods and to attend to the predominant moods and emotions experienced in the relationship. This means observing how the moods and emotions enhance or detract from the quality of conversations (and influence those that do not occur). In Part Five, I will share more about the interdependence between our moods and the quality of our conversations.

The three dimensions relevant to our 'way of doing' as a team

1. Coordination of action

Teams exist to accomplish what individuals working separately cannot. How teams coordinate action is at the heart of organisational work and the associated successes or failures. The specialist and diverse nature of work means that coordinating separate efforts is crucial for producing satisfactory outcomes and realising goals and objectives. When coordination breaks down, performance and productivity suffer, tension increases and strain is placed on relationships.

2. Conversations

The conversations that do (and don't) happen and the quality of those conversations is fundamental to the context of effective working relationships. There's a growing recognition that the ability to handle difficult conversations and discuss the undiscussable are prerequisites to organisational change and success. This requires us all to cultivate a mindset and an environment that facilitates sharing of information and together making the most informed choices to achieve better results.

What we say and don't say, how we say it, how we are listened to, and what happens to team members emotionally when words are spoken, are crucial to efficient and effective team performance. The quality of the conversational networks is a major determinant of the team's morale, performance and productivity.

Conversations that do not generate new insights or innovative practices, inform actions or generate positive results are unproductive; they create and perpetuate costly communication breakdowns and waste.

3. Alignment

Where there is alignment between two parties, they are committed to going in the same direction. This implies they agree on the direction and what is being worked towards. It also includes agreement about the key steps to getting there. Alignment includes a commitment to being collaborative and coordinating action. Equally important, however, is stating what one feels is missing as a reflection of one's commitment to wanting to remain aligned.

DISCIPLINE #4: DELIVER OUR RESULTS

'An individual can make a difference,
but a team makes a miracle.'
—Doug Pederson, Head Coach of the Philadelphia
Eagles after winning the 2018 Super Bowl LII

A team exists to achieve what no other entity in the organisation can. For a team to succeed, it has to have a clear understanding of its performance goals. Consider what teams could accomplish if they were to operate at more than the sum of their parts for 30%–40% of the time. While we appreciate this is difficult, it is possible. The *rewards* of success will always outweigh the *costs* of success.

Why do most teams operate at less than the sum of their parts if they have the potential to access the collective capacity and capability? When I ask teams what percentage of the time they believe they perform and operate at less than, equal to or more than the sum of their parts, the answers are consistently similar:

- 10%–20% of the time: more than the sum of their parts.
- 50% of the time: equal to the sum of their parts.
- 30%–40% of the time: less than the sum of their parts.

The team's results

What prevents teams from operating at their best, unlocking their inherent power and accessing their collective capacity and capability? Peter Senge says, '... you come across teams with an average intelligence of over 120, but the team functions at a collective intelligence of about 60.'

Research tells us that teams who do not confirm their stakeholders' mandate and have no unifying purpose or agreed ways of working will consistently operate at less than the sum of their parts. They are no more than a group of leaders who are only interested in their own goals and who work separately from their colleagues. Jon Katzenbach says that 'Real teams are deeply committed to their purpose, approach and collective goals.'

Teams achieve what no other entity in the organisation can. High performing teams co-create and carry out their work together by holding themselves individually and collectively accountable for achieving certain performance goals that can only be achieved by working interdependently. High performing teams focus their individual and collective capacity and capabilities on delivering great work that facilitates transformational change to the benefit of all stakeholders.

Teams deliver value and bring about transformational change by committing to the responses to these questions:

1. What great work is the team commissioned to accomplish?

2. What specific collective performance goals does the team hold itself accountable for and which ones can only be achieved by working interdependently?

3. What actions will the team commit to and what measures will assess the team's success against each goal?

The following key themes and indicators are worth noting:

- What gets rewarded gets done. It is no coincidence that the lowest scoring indicator in the *5 Disciplines of a High Performing Team Assessment* highlights the reality across most teams: financial and other rewards are biased towards individual contribution rather than being team-based / collective achievements. Until organisations address this imbalance, individual team members will be inclined to focus on accomplishing what will yield the greatest reward. It's human nature. Organisations need to provide simpler ways to measure and reward 'team contribution'.

- Make meetings matter. Research undertaken by the Harvard Business School showed that:

  - 71% of leaders believe meetings are unproductive and inefficient.

  - 65% of leaders said meetings keep them from completing their own work.

  - 64% of leaders said meetings come at the expense of deep thinking.

  - 62% of leaders said meetings miss opportunities to bring the team closer together.

  Leaders spend, on average, between 50% and 60% of their time in meetings; therefore, how their time, energy and attention is managed and channelled is essential to how teams perform.

- Performance is at the heart of what matters for teams—no team can arise without a performance challenge. A team's performance ethic is a function of its clarity and commitment to a common set of performance goals. Most team members' primary focus is on achieving individual KPIs, which is an inhibitor to being a high performance team. This siloed mentality results from a lack of clear and committed collective performance goals.

- German philosopher Peter Sloterdijk talks about the trap of 'hysterical industriousness'. He says we have a 'tendency to be habituated to a continual fast pace of life, endeavoring to cope with demands and pressures with no time for anything.'

  I believe 'hysterical industriousness' is the root cause of much of the dissatisfaction and frustration experienced across organisations today. The pride so many share in their level of busyness (always in a hurry, multi-tasking, swamped by emails, attending pointless meetings) leaves them with little or no time or energy to do anything other than react to what's in front of them. It's no wonder leadership teams are not engaging with employees as 'transformational leaders', but rather 'reactive doers'.

- The whole is greater than the sum of its parts. On the one hand, it's expected that team members recognise the outcomes of a team are better than any individual could arrive at by themselves. To recognise this, however, doesn't guarantee teams realise the value in it. Recognising the power of the collective is at least a starting point.

How teams coordinate action

Let's turn our attention to what is required for teams to co-create. There are three elements that underpin a team's ability and capacity to deliver results:

1. The distinction between bad, good and great work.
2. Clarity of a team's performance goals.
3. How to coordinate action, together.

Bad, good and great work

In his book, *Do More Great Work,* Michael Bungay Stanier shared, 'Everything we do falls into one of three buckets – it's either bad work, good work or great work.' He is referring to the meaning and impact the work has on those performing the work and recipients of the work. He goes on to explain that bad work is work that wastes time, energy and effort. Doing this work once is one time too many. It is pointless work. Sadly, the truth is we generally do more bad work than we care to admit or know. Bad work is like comfort food: it's easy, it provides a false sense of satisfaction and there is a price to pay from engaging in it.

It shows up in bureaucratic red tape (few see reason for it and no one benefits from it) and in meetings where you can't ascertain its purpose, what is being discussed or agreed upon, and where it's unclear as to what is to be done by whom by when. Bad work shows up in outdated processes that waste everyone's time and in ways of doing things that add no value, have no impact and offer even less meaning. Think about the time and effort it takes to produce reports: Who reads them? What do they need them for? What would happen if they weren't done?

Most of us find it hard to admit we do much bad work. Once we observe and critically examine how we spend our time, we are amazed by how much of it is wasted doing bad work. Have a go—you may just find you have more time and energy to do more fulfilling and purposeful work.

Work	Type	Nature	Value
Great	New ways of working	'Transformational' (Strategic focus)	High value, high impact with long term benefits
Good	Ways of working that embody best practice	'Running' (Operational and tactical focus)	Necessary work to get short and medium term results
Bad	Habituated, senseless routines	Reactive	Low value, wasteful

Teams are typically more familiar with good work as it's the work with which they are best equipped to do well—they have the skills, knowledge and experience. Doing good work takes up most of a team's time and there's nothing wrong with that. Good work comes from what one has been taught to do, as well as from the ongoing training required to maintain levels of required performance. At one end, it can be engaging and interesting, and at the other, it can be mundane. But it is recognised as necessary and most are willing to spend time and energy doing it. Good work is a source of success.

Teams who engage in good work distinguish themselves by how they manage their cost base and protect the profit margin by ensuring the most efficient processes and systems are used to enhance levels of productivity. Change is facilitated through a disciplined approach and application of change-managed principles and practices.

At an organisational level, good work is vital. It is a company's bread and butter—the efficient, focused, profitable work that delivers the next quarterly results.

Great work is meaningful. It has an impact on you and others; it makes a difference. It inspires, stretches and provokes. Great work is the work that matters. It is a source of deep comfort and engagement where you feel 'in flow'—time stands still and you're working at your best, effortlessly. The comfort comes from its connection; it's what is most meaningful to you—not only your core values and beliefs but your aspirations and hopes for the impact you want to have on the world.

However, great work is also a place of uncertainty and discomfort. The discomfort arises because the work is often new and challenging, and this presents an element of risk and possible failure.

For organisations, great work drives strategic difference, innovation and longevity. Often, this kind of inventive work pushes businesses forward and leads to new products, more efficient systems and increased profits.

To do more great work, teams need to do less bad work.

I worked with an executive leadership team who came to recognise that approximately 40% of its time (as individuals and collectively) was spent doing bad work. Here are some examples of bad work, good work and great work that were identified.

Bad work the team committed to stop doing:

- Meetings with no clear purpose, no pre-set agenda and no understanding of what participants are expected to prepare or looked upon to contribute.

- Meetings where circular conversations persist, no decisions are taken and no plan of action or responsibilities are assigned.

- Making decisions that can't be made due to incomplete data or data that lacks the requisite integrity.

- Accepting poor performance from colleagues and team members.

- Commitments that are not fulfilled and where no prior notice or justifiable reasons are given.

- Time taken up by unnecessary distractions like emails that are labelled urgent.

- Conversations that fail to address what is most important.

- Procrastination over making important decisions.

- Lack of communication resulting in being blindsided by situations that could have been avoided.

- Time wasted making 'sloppy requests' of others and committing to sloppy requests from others.

Good work the team committed to continue doing:

- Providing clarity of expectation and securing others' commitment to deliver expected outcomes.

- Delivering to budgetary expectations and engaging in meaningful forecasting processes.

- Engaging with customers and proactive stakeholder management.

- Informing, consulting and involving others where relevant.

- Learning with and from one another and understanding the contributory factors to both the successes and failures.

- Seeking clarity of expectation before committing to action.

- Continuous scanning for improvement opportunities in processes and systems to ensure greater efficiencies.

- Collaborating with key stakeholders and being aware of the impact decisions have on others.

- Focusing on the health and wellbeing of staff and ensuring a motivational environment exists for people to learn in and do good work.

- Enhancing brand uniqueness and positioning.

Great work the team committed to start or do more of:

- Investing time in coaching and developing others to realise their potential.

- Engaging in longer term 'Horizon 3' planning and deliver on the transformational agenda.

- Engaging in out-of-the-box thinking to explore new markets and business opportunities.

- Deep engagement and collaboration on transformational projects: setting clear objectives and reviewing progress.

- Stress testing new ideas and opportunities.

- Continuously setting clearer and higher expectations and guidelines.

- Engaging in external forums and events to gain new learning and accessing new thinking and ideas.

- Spending more time interacting with valued clients and partners (suppliers).

- Identifying and developing potential successors for all executive roles.

- Simplification of business processes and practices.

- Developing deeper commercial insights and acumen.

The team also committed to ensuring and managing its time based on allocating:

- Less than 10% of its time doing bad work.

- 60% of its time delivering good work.

- 30% of its time thinking about and accomplishing great work.

The most important steps the team took were identifying, agreeing and committing to the collective performance goals for which they held themselves mutually accountable and which could only be achieved by working interdependently.

The team's performance goals

Teams are energised by significant performance goals. These performance goals provide opportunities to deliver exceptional customer service and value, and provide invaluable learning and growth opportunities for team members and others involved in their development, planning and delivery. Ultimately, achieving performance goals that deliver exceptional value is likely to deliver a return to shareholders and provide attractive earning opportunities for team members and employees.

Why then, given that they are so powerful, do many teams fail to access their collective capacity and capability and not operate at more than the sum of their parts? I believe there are three common reasons:

1. First is the lack of clarity of the team's collective performance goals and outcomes to be achieved. Where goals are not clearly defined and the measure of success is not clearly identified, it becomes difficult to secure the team's commitment and cooperation. Where the results to be achieved are not shared or understood by the entire team and are not aligned to the organisation's strategic objectives, teams fragment and deliver suboptimal results.

    As Lencioni shows in his model of the five dysfunctions of a team, 'inattention to results' is followed by an avoidance of accountability due to a lack of commitment.

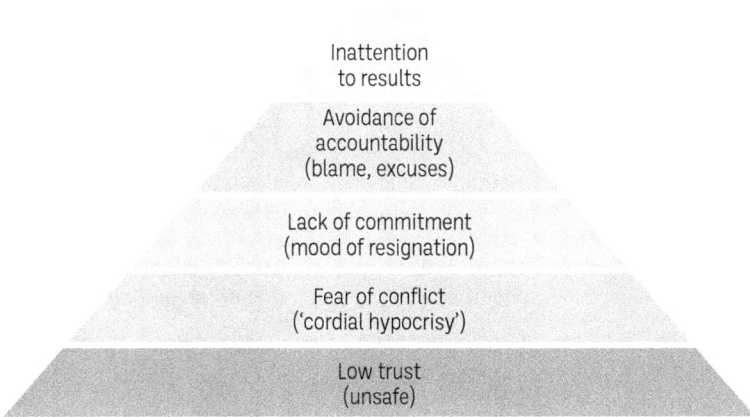

Inattention
to results

Avoidance of
accountability
(blame, excuses)

Lack of commitment
(mood of resignation)

Fear of conflict
('cordial hypocrisy')

Low trust
(unsafe)

2. Second is that teams fail to work on both the operational and transformational agendas in parallel. Teams need to balance directing their collective energy to deal with current challenges and create space to consider and anticipate future challenges. Teams who develop the capacity to seamlessly shift their attention and energy from the 'dance floor' to the 'balcony' differentiate themselves as high performing teams.

In today's 'always on', fast-paced environment, teams increasingly feel like they operate in permanent white water: facing increasing complexity, uncertainty and rapid change. In such circumstances, team members are less able to discern between what is most important and less important; they don't know where to focus and maintain their attention. Working relationships often deteriorate and they remain stuck in recurring, limiting behavioural patterns that produce suboptimal results.

Running and Transforming our business

Business Imperatives	GOOD WORK 'Operational Priorities'	GREAT WORK 'Transformational Imperative'
Strategic intent	Cost, profit focus	Innovation, growth focus
Critical tasks	Operations, efficiency, incremental innovation	Adaptability and breakthrough innovation
Competencies	Operational domain specific	Entrepreneurial, enterprise thinking
Structure	Formal, hierarchy, centralised, controlling	Dynamic, fluid, integrated network of teams
Controls, rewards	Margins, productivity	Milestones and growth
Culture	Efficiency, low risk, quality, customers, problem reactive	Risk taking, speed, flexibility, experimentation, solution creative
Leadership role	Management 'over' – knowledge, process system – 'top down'	Leadership 'with' – purpose, relational, visionary, collective, distributed, collaborative

Consider your team meetings: How much time is devoted to thinking, discussing and addressing operational and transformational priorities? Do team meeting agendas reflect an appropriate allocation of time and importance to 'running' and 'transforming' the business? What portion of each team member's own time and attention is given to the running priorities and transformational imperatives? Their diaries will answer this question.

3. Third is the imbalance between individual responsibility and collective accountability. Most of us have grown

up with a strong sense of individualism. For much of our upbringing, we are evaluated, recognised and rewarded above collective success when it comes to formal education, professional careers and individual accomplishments. We are taught to believe that if we don't take care of our own interests, no one else will. While this may be true for some facets of our lives, it can make it difficult for some team members to reconcile risking achieving individual accomplishments and rewards over pursuing collective goals over which they feel they have less direct influence.

As Jon Katzenbach shared, 'Self-preservation and individual accountability can work two ways. Left unattended, they can preclude or destroy teams. But recognised and addressed for what they are, especially if done with reference to how to meet a performance challenge, individual concerns and differences become a source of collective strengths.' Teams are not an antithesis to individual prowess. Teams comprise individuals who, upon accessing their collective capacity and capability, come to achieve the greatest things possible.

Aligning a team to a set of performance goals need not be a complicated process. I would encourage the following two-step process:

1. Invite team members to identify what they each believe to be the three most important performance goals (individually and collectively) for the next twelve months. Do not limit them to three goals; however, as a starting point, it is recommended that you encourage greater discernment between what is most important for the team to commit to over individual goals. In addition, for

each of the three goals, identify the critical measures and outcomes to assess progress and success towards accomplishing each. Establishing a clear line of sight to the end goal will align team energy and buy-in to each goal. See diagram below:

What – our collective performance goals

Those goals we collectively own and can only achieve, working interdependently

Our ExLT Collective GOALS	Outcomes and measures
1.	• Outcomes and Measures • Outcomes and Measures • Outcomes and Measures
2.	• Outcomes and Measures • Outcomes and Measures • Outcomes and Measures
3.	• Outcomes and Measures • Outcomes and Measures • Outcomes and Measures

2. Once the team agrees on three goals, break down each goal into tasks, timelines and responsibilities. Keeping the 'plan on a page' helps bring greater clarity and focus. A goal without a plan is no more than a wish. Below is a Hoshin planning template. It was developed in Japan over 50 years ago but has become widely recognised across the world as the most effective way to think, plan, implement and review progress towards accomplishing goals.

TEAM – COLLECTIVE PERFORMANCE GOAL						
Goal:						
Objective	Action Plan	Who	When			
			Q1	Q2	Q3	Q4
Target/Goals:		Key messages to employees:				
Sponsor:	Estimated Benefits:					
Project Team:	Financial:					
	Budget and Resource Requirement:					
Measures KPI:						

How teams coordinate action to achieve the greatest possible outcomes

Teams are about getting things done smoothly and successfully. Given the normality of uncertainty, our flow of work is subject to disruptions and interferences that require us to continually adapt and adjust. How teams adapt and secure one another's cooperation and commitment is fundamental to effectively coordinating action.

To illustrate, let me share a conversation I had with an executive with whom I engaged in an executive coaching relationship. For anonymity, I will call him John.

At the height of the COVID-19 pandemic, John, like most leaders, faced a significant challenge: how could he ensure that teams across the organisation continued to perform and deliver results while working remotely?

Over a Zoom call, John shared a concern. 'Pre-COVID, we were all teaming and working together in the office. Now, in this hybrid way of working, we're working together and apart with half the team members working from the office and the other half working from home.'

Sensing there was a greater underlying concern, I asked what concerned him most about working remotely.

John replied, 'Well, I'm not sure that we are coordinating action as effectively as we could. If I'm really honest, I'm not sure that the team members are as productive as they could be, and in fact, I'm a little concerned that they're wasting a lot of time.'

Curious as to what was on John's mind, I asked how he believed team members were wasting their time. 'We're having too many unproductive meetings. So much effort goes into staying engaged in back-to-back virtual meetings day after day. Outside of that, everyone is getting caught up with distractions around the house and I've no doubt that some are watching movies on Netflix.'

While this may have been the case, I couldn't help but think about what this may indicate about the levels of trust across the organisation. Reflecting on John's response, I offered a different perspective and suggested that besides the 'known spoken' concerns he raised, there was also a range of 'known unspoken' concerns. I suggested that one of the most significant 'known unspoken' breakdowns to coordinating action was the propensity team members have to make sloppy requests of others.

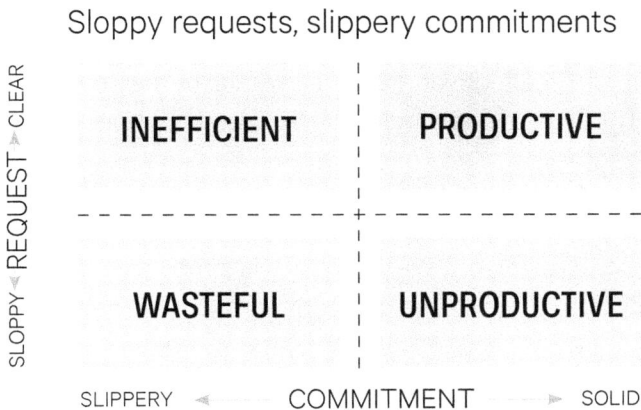

Sloppy requests, slippery commitments

	SLIPPERY ← COMMITMENT → SOLID	
CLEAR (REQUEST)	INEFFICIENT	PRODUCTIVE
SLOPPY (REQUEST)	WASTEFUL	UNPRODUCTIVE

We make sloppy requests of others when we do the following:

1. When we throw out hints but don't ask for anything specific, for example, 'your desk needs a clean.'

2. When the precise nature of actions to be performed is not specified, for example, 'could you tidy your desk?'

3. When the exact time to have the task completed by is not indicated, for example, your desk needs to be tidied as soon as possible.'

4. The criteria to judge satisfactory completion is not clear, for example, 'everything is to be neat.'

5. The assumption that the listener understands the precise nature of what has been requested.

As Alan Sieler in *Coaching to the Human Soul* says, 'a sloppy request will always get a slippery commitment.'

Consider for a moment how much time and effort is wasted by making and committing to sloppy requests. How teams coordinate action to achieve what is most important is a function of the effectiveness of the requests they make of one another and the quality and trust in the commitments they give to one another.

I asked John how many requests, on average, he made of others on any given day—be they via email, voicemail or in direct conversation. After some thought, John estimated he made 40–50 requests of others each day. I then asked him to consider what percentage of his requests were fully met to his satisfaction. He answered that on average only 40%–60% of his requests were fully met.

The sad truth is that John isn't the exception. The results from a poll I conducted in 2020 also showed that between 40% and

60% of requests made of others are effectively met. Imagine the implications across an organisation when, on average, 50% of requests made of others are not satisfactorily met.

Imagine the dollar value of the direct and indirect costs associated with 50% of everyone's requests not being met? How much time, effort and energy are being wasted by having to make the same request of others and them having to redo the work. Besides the wasted time and energy, what impact would this have on the levels of morale and motivation across the organisation?

DISCIPLINE #5: DEVELOP OUR LEARNING

High performing teams differentiate themselves by their uncompromising responsibility for each other's learning, growth and success. They seek and are open to learning with and from each other. This way they can examine the reasons for their successes and the causes of their failures.

Flourishing teams share a tireless commitment to build the team's collective wisdom, which enables it to leverage greater collective capacity and capability. Collaborative and high performing teams are curious; they are open to seeing things differently, identifying new opportunities, taking risks and experimenting with new ways of doing things. They collaborate on ideas, insights and intuition. They are never not learning.

High performing teams grow their collective wisdom by sharing insights to these questions:

1. What do we appreciate about how we contributed to our success?

2. What patterns of thinking and behaviour prevent us from operating at our best?

3. What do we commit to learning more about? And what changes can we make to be a more effective and high performing team?

The team's learning

Life is uncertain. In our daily routines and rhythms of life, we continuously have to deal with unanticipated interruptions and interferences: breakdowns to the habitual flow and cadence of life.

Teams are never not in breakdown (having to deal with unanticipated interruptions and interferences). Winning a new tender for a scale of project never previously undertaken represents a positive breakdown. Such a positive breakdown may present varied challenges in terms of project management capability and the need to hire new and more skilled team members. Conversely, teams may experience negative breakdowns: the loss of key team members critical to the team's capacity to deliver on its commitments.

Despite how a team assesses the impact of a breakdown, team members must adapt and adjust. The essence of adapting is learning. As Alan Sieler shares, 'Adapting is not about coping individually, but about learning to cope together.'

Our existing skills, knowledge and experience will help overcome the challenge or address the problem. However, given the increasing levels of uncertainty and complexity of the world in which we live and work, our existing skills, knowledge and experience may not be sufficient. In such cases, we need access to different domains of learning. For example, COVID-19 represents a collective global breakdown, which has required nations, leaders, scientists and other parties to collaborate to find new solutions beyond the limits of existing knowledge, practice and understanding to contain and reduce transmission as well as to treat and save the lives of those affected by the disease.

Learning happens in action and from thinking. When we adapt our thinking we access new possibilities.

As humans, our very survival depends upon our ability to adapt, evolve and grow. Teams and organisations are living, dynamic systems with an inherent capacity to evolve and to achieve more than is believed possible.

Learning is a social process that involves reflection and dialogue.

The four interdependent domains of learning

According to Peter Senge, learning organisations are, '... organisations where people continually expand their capacity to create the results they truly desire, where new and expansive patterns of thinking are nurtured, where collective aspiration is set free, and where people are continually learning to see the whole together.'

In his ground-breaking book, *The Fifth Discipline*, Senge proposes that for teams to deal with increasing levels of complexity and change, they need to be flexible and adaptable and, most importantly, be able to tap into 'people's commitment and capacity to learn at all (four) levels.'

1. Personal mastery

Organisations learn through individuals; however, not all of what individuals learn is necessarily of value to organisations. Individual learning needs to go beyond developing competence and technical expertise to include deepened levels of self-awareness, a sense of purpose and an ability to adapt one's thinking. Senge says, 'People with a high level of personal mastery are acutely aware of their ignorance, their incompetence, and their growth areas.'

2. Mental models

Part of being human is to live in assessment of and about ourselves and others. We are never not in the story of how we see the world and the meaning we make of our experiences in the world. As Anaïs Nin, the famous French novelist, once said, 'We don't see the world as it is, we see it as we are.' To learn is to observe our assessments and to reflect on how they may not serve us. What assessment would better serve us to access new possibilities?

3. Building a shared vision

One of the most distinguishing attributes of effective leaders and teams is to inspire a greater sense of purpose and a shared vision of what is possible. Effective, high performing teams know that the cause they serve is greater than themselves. They create a vision that inspires others to be more curious and to develop greater courage to experiment and innovate. Senge says, 'When there is a genuine vision (as opposed to the all-too-familiar "vision statement"), people excel and learn, not because they are told to, but because they want to.'

4. Team learning

A team is different from a group in that team members not only take responsibility for their own learning, growth and evolvement but also for each other's. They share an unwavering commitment to grow the collective wisdom captured from how they individually and collectively contribute to their successes and failures. Learning happens in conversation: a dialogue. As a team, team members share and advocate their individual insights and perspectives and inquire as to how others see things. They inquire in order to understand others, rather than be in judgement of others.

Alan Sieler distinguishes between 'first order learning' and 'second order learning'. At its essence, first order learning stems from the belief that our behaviour determines the results we get. Therefore, in order to get a different result we need to change our behaviour. This explains why some people believe that in order to be heard, you need to shout louder. While this may work sometimes, it's not guaranteed to work all the time. No learning happens from shouting louder.

Let's turn our attention to second order learning. Take a moment to reflect on a recent challenge where you would have made matters worse if you had dealt with it in your usual way. Why does this happen? It's because we are limited by how we see things. Let's go back to the previous example. If I continue to 'see' it as wrong that others do not listen to me, I'm likely to continue to believe it's best to shout louder.

What is learning?

1. What opinions would better serve me?
2. What mood would better serve me?

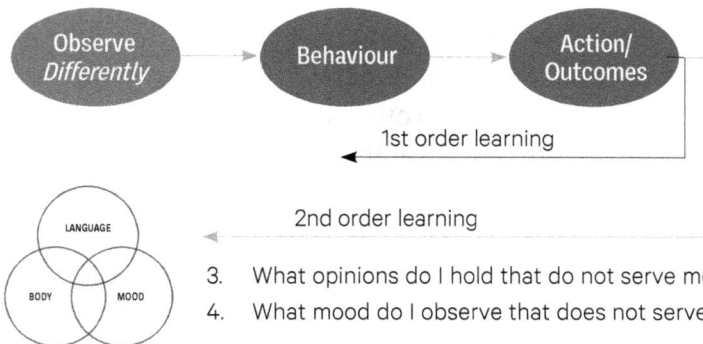

3. What opinions do I hold that do not serve me?
4. What mood do I observe that does not serve me?

Second order learning is about being a different observer: to observe the world (and ourselves) differently. Only when we are open to seeing things differently will new possibilities arise. As Seth Godin said, 'If your audience isn't listening, it's not their fault. It's yours.' Second order learning requires us to ask ourselves, 'how may I be contributing to others choosing not to listen?' Second order learning is about being a different observer. It is the commitment you make to being a better and different observer of yourself. Essentially, this is the ability to observe the assessment you hold of yourself and the predominant mood you are in that may limit your ability to see things differently.

Second order learning involves being a diligent observer and asking yourself how you may have contributed to this situation occurring in ways you previously did not see. Let's revert to the concern of not being listened to. As a different observer of oneself, you may come to the realisation that you seldom ask others for their opinion and spend most of the time asserting your opinion. This may be difficult to acknowledge but is invaluable in opening up different possibilities other than believing the only option is to shout louder.

How teams learn with and from one another

Teams survive and strive based on how effectively they learn. A team's ability to learn is shaped by its members' capacity to be flexible and adaptable in the face of increasing levels of uncertainty and unpredictability. This, therefore, requires team members to reflect on how they are as learners and what they could do differently to become better learners.

1. Enemies and allies of learning

As a first step, team members need to be open to exploring what Alan Sieler calls our 'enemies and allies of learning'. Enemies of learning are those aspects that hinder or block our ability to learn. Allies of learning are those aspects that greatly enhance and enable us to be effective learners. Allies of learners open us to the possibility to see things differently and adapt and adjust how we act to better deal with the unanticipated interruptions of our daily lives.

Enemies of learning (Source: Newfield Institute): Reflect on these obstacles to learning and identify the five you recognise most consistently present themselves to you.

Enemies of learning	Applicable
I don't know what I don't know—cognitive blindness.	
I don't admit or am unwilling to admit that I don't know.	
I don't want to admit that someone else knows.	
I confuse knowing with having an opinion.	
I confuse knowing with having the truth—'I'm right.'	
Self-doubt and lack of confidence.	
Trapped in the judgements of others—'I have to get it right.'	
Comparing myself to others and thinking negatively of myself.	
Jumping to conclusions—assess everything and thus am not open to new possibilities.	
Too busy to learn—'I don't have the time.'	
Mood of significance—'I'm ok. It's others that need it more.'	
Arrogance—not prepared to unlearn; too attached to existing knowledge.	
Lack of patience—'I want it now.'	
Contaminated with the need of certainty—have to be clear all the time and get it right.	

Enemies of learning	Applicable
Anxiety—fear I will not be good enough.	
Being caught in the mood of confusion rather than curiosity.	
Not taking time to reflect and apply learning.	
Not taking care of my health and energy—too tired to learn.	
Being driven by novelty—just scratch the surface, unwilling to persist.	

What must you commit to change to overcome your 'enemies of learning'?

Allies of learning (Source: Newfield Institute)**:** Reflect on what you could do to ensure you are more open to learning. Which of the following present the greatest opportunities?

Allies of learning	Applicable
Declaration of ignorance—'I don't know.'	
Declaration of being a learner—'I don't know and I want to be a learner.'	
Declaring to be a 'teacher'—'I can and want to learn from this person.'	
Declaration of legitimacy as a learner—'I'm not perfect and I am a learner.'	
Making a request—'Could you please help me learn this?'	
Declaring emotions as an important domain for learning.	
Humility—'Who would be in the best position to help me?'	
Curiosity and wonder—'I wonder what could be if I were to ... '	
Acceptance and patience—'I can't know it all, so let me keep at it.'	
Courage—'It's totally acceptable to not know or not have the answer.'	
Staying with being uncomfortable and unsettled about new perspectives and experiences.	

Allies of learning	Applicable
Determination and persistence—'I will do all I can to explore all possible options.'	
Lightness and the ability to laugh at myself (Rule #6: Don't take things too seriously.)	
Being passionate but not obsessive about finding a way through the issue.	
Accepting how it feels not to know or have certainty.	
Being more observant. Being mindful of what I'm thinking and feeling but not saying it. Asking if what I think and feel is helping or hindering my learning.	

What must you commit to change to embrace your 'allies of learning'?

2. Be open to give and receive feedback

To learn means being willing to admit to what we don't know, being open to seeing what we are blind to and recognising the gap between our aspired and actual levels of performance. Learning happens in conversation; it is a social process that involves reflection and dialogue.

Being open to asking for and receiving feedback, and committing to learning from it, is at the core of being an effective learner. For teams to learn, a safe and supportive space must be created. Only then will team members give themselves permission to be vulnerable to seek and courageously offer feedback. When team members are open to what they 'don't know' and curious to 'want to know', learning is possible. In our increasingly competitive world, the constant need to know, to be right and to win could paradoxically become our undoing. As Fred Kofman says in *Conscious Business*, 'Learning must be prized, not merely tolerated – the culture of the knower must give way to the culture of the learner; otherwise, we will become the culture of the left-behinds.'

Declare yourself a beginner

Having reflected on both the enemies and allies of learning and made a commitment to become a more effective learner, I invite you to declare yourself a 'beginner'. This in no way 'illegitimises' what one knows; rather, it opens us up to learning about what we don't know.

Feedback is crucial. Feedforward is vital. Research by Sheila Heen and Douglas Stone showed that 63% of cited managers were unable or unwilling to have the 'difficult' feedback conversations. While much has been written and taught on how to provide feedback, less is offered on how to receive feedback. Learning happens in reflection: through feedback from others' assessment of one's past behaviour. To learn from feedback requires us to be vulnerable.

Learning also happens from recommendations: feedforward from others. Feedforward enables us to assess a situation differently or understand what different ways we could deal with or manage a difficult situation. To learn from feedforward requires us to be curious.

For feedback to be effective, there are five critical steps team members need to follow:

How to learn from feedback

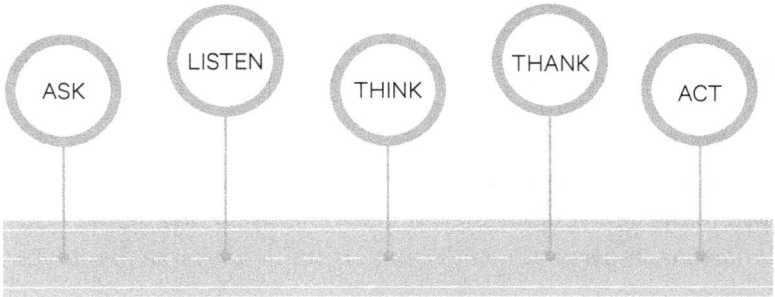

ASK   LISTEN   THINK   THANK   ACT

First, you need to **ask for feedback.** Ask, not with the intent to validate what you already know but to learn what you may not know.

Second, **listen to the feedback.** It is crucial that you listen to understand rather than defend yourself against what is being said.

Third, **think about the feedback**. Think about what new learning and possibilities the feedback could elicit. Be aware of any resistance in your listening that may prevent or block potential learning. Be curious.

Fourth, **thank the person for the feedback**. This does not mean you need to agree with what they said but to acknowledge their preparedness to provide the feedback. Acknowledging others for their feedback creates a safer and more supportive learning environment.

Finally, **act on the feedback.** Share what you commit to change and secure others' ongoing support to help you remain accountable.

As leadership thinker Marshall Goldsmith said, 'By asking for feedback, analyzing the results, developing a focused action plan for change and following-up, leaders are perceived as more effective.'

The following six steps (outlined by Heen and Stone) can help team members better receive feedback:

1. Observe the tendencies

Are team members prone to being defensive or arguing about the method used to collect the feedback? Do they default to making excuses or striking back at the feedback? Do they first reject it but later consider it and accept it?

2. Disentangle the 'what' from the 'who'

Do team members attack the messenger or attend to the message? It doesn't matter who delivers the message; what matters is the message that's sent. It's critical that team members separate the message from the messenger.

3. Sort towards coaching

Some feedback is evaluative; it is based on ratings and on others' judgement. Both matter. Do team members see the value in others' assessments and are they open to being coached by their peers?

3. Unpack the feedback

Sometimes the message is hidden or lost in translation: how we hear it is not what the person delivering it intended. Do team members seek clarity or do they act on untested assumptions based on what they 'knew' the other person meant? Are team members proactive? Do they test how the message has been understood?

4. Ask for just one thing

Less is more. Do team members offer or seek the most important or beneficial learning others could provide?

5. Engage in small experiments

Learning happens in action. Nothing changes until something changes, so take action. Do team members share their intentions (what they could, may or possibly do differently) or their commitments (what they will or have done differently)? Learning happens through action, not intention.

The gifts of 1's and 5's

Most of us consider ourselves above average. This is more so the case when we assess ourselves on a scale of 1 to 10. Why is this so? Well, psychologists call it 'illusory superiority'. David Dunning, author of *Self-Insight,* believes that illusory superiority '... happens for many reasons, two of which are others are too polite to say what they really think and incompetent people lack the skills to assess their abilities accurately.'

One of the most effective ways to mitigate the effects of illusory superiority and to ensure feedback is of the greatest value is to share the gifts of 1's and 5's. A rating of 3 on a 5-point scale is often a meaningless and unhelpful rating of oneself or another. It says nothing. There's no learning in rating average. Learning happens at the edges: where a rating of 1 represents the greatest opportunity for change and improvement, and 5 represents a strength to be leveraged. So, when you are next asked to rate yourself or are invited to rate another, share the gifts of 1's and 5's.

This is not to suggest that every indicator ought to be rated a 1 or a 5. If a questionnaire has 20 indicators, find at least three gifts each of 1 and 5. When sharing feedback, provide examples to illustrate what you mean and how you came to the rating. Ensure the other person understands the language you use to explain the rating.

As Arie de Geus, author of *The Living Company,* reminds us, 'An organisation's ability to learn faster than its competitor is the only source of sustainable competitive advantage.'

COMING UP IN PART FOUR

Transitioning from a floundering or functional team to a flourishing, high performing team is possible. Any endeavour in pursuit of our individual and collective potential is difficult. It's why it rarely happens. When teams make the choice and commit to access more of their greatness, anything is possible. It's how man came to walk on the moon; it's how a COVID vaccine was developed in 8 months not 15 years—the average time it takes to commercialise a vaccine—and it's how Apple has achieved a market value of $1trillion.

To begin unlocking the power in the team you lead and to access more of the collective capacity and capability, let's focus on how your team is teaming.

Data I've collected from the past 10 years as a leadership team coach reveals much about what is possible when teams flourish.

Part Four
What is happening

5 Disciplines of High Performing Teams Assessment

In Part Four, we explore the data accumulated from the conversations conducted with team leaders and team members over many years. It provides an analysis of the scores and comments collected from the *5 Disciplines of High Performing Teams Assessment* that teams undertake during the Discovery Phase prior to commencing the Team Coaching Program. (Details of the Team Coaching Program will be covered in Part Six.)

WHAT WE DISCOVERED

As a team coach, I have had the privilege to work with leadership teams across a wide range of industry sectors including public and private companies and government agencies. Common to all those teams was their undeniable commitment to unlocking their inherent power and accessing their collective capacity and capability to achieve the greatest possible outcomes for their stakeholders.

Before the commencement of the Team Coaching Program, the discovery phase establishes an understanding of each team member's perspectives and insights into how they experience being part of the team and what they appreciate about the strengths the team represents. It also offers an opportunity to understand how individual team members believe they collectively contribute to the team's success and any patterns of thinking and behaviour that limit and hinder the team's ability to operate. The discovery phase serves as an essential process to securing an aligned understanding of what success would look like for the team and to secure each team member's commitment and ownership to the outcomes of the learning journey.

Team members complete an assessment based on the *5 Disciplines of High Performing Teams Assessment*. The assessment is centred on 18 indicators distributed across the 5 Disciplines:

Discover	Declare (Purpose)	Design (Dynamics)	Deliver	Develop
1. The team has a clear mandate from its stakeholders.	1. Team members understand, can articulate and are committed to the team's purpose.	1. The team behaviours and shared 'ways of working' have been identified and are consistently upheld.	1. The team has clear collective performance goals and success criteria which can be achieved only by working interdependently.	1. Team members are open to receiving and giving feedback to each other on their performance and behaviours.
2. The team relates well to all its key stakeholders with the team members representing the whole team.	2. Team members know and consistently uphold the team's values.	2. The team members secure cooperation and commitment from each other.	2. Achieving the team's goals is recognised and rewarded above achieving individual goals.	2. Team members support each other and are committed to each other's ongoing learning and development.
3. The team has been selected to have the complementary skills to achieve its mandate.		3. Team members are equally accountable for their own areas of responsibility and the team's collective goals.	3. The outcomes achieved are better than any individual could arrive at by themselves.	3. Team members keep challenging themselves and others to keep developing and adding greater value.
		4. All team members are engaged and involved, and the team uses of its diversity.	4. Team members leave meetings feeling more focused, supported, and energised.	
			5. The team scans its stakeholders' environment and constantly attends to changing needs and perceptions.	
			6. Team members engage employees at all levels as transformational leaders.	

DATA ANALYSIS FROM 5 DISCIPLINES OF HIGH PERFORMING TEAMS ASSESSMENT

How teams are

The following scale represents where teams are in the different operating styles:

a. Collaborative teams score above the 85th percentile.

b. Cohesive teams range between the 70th and the 84th percentile.

c. Competitive teams range between the 50th and the 69th percentile.

d. Combative teams range from 0 to the 50th percentile.

The data shows eight key findings:

1. Competitive is the predominant team operating style

The mean score of 6.73 across all 5 Disciplines suggests that most teams shift between a Competitive and a Cohesive operating style and rarely demonstrate a Collaborative style. When a team does collaborate, it is on matters to which the team feels more aligned and to what it most agrees on. Seldom would the team collaborate to explore the possibilities in its conflicting views and perspectives on more complex matters. More typically, the team members would feel that:

a. The levels of trust within the team are not where they need to be.

b. It's not safe to challenge or criticise each other's thinking as team members react defensively rather than remaining open to being influenced by one another.

c. Decisions are often deferred but when made, buy-in and commitment are not equally shared.

d. Meetings are less productive as personal agendas and self-interest are never far from the team members' thinking and feelings.

e. Seldom does the team operate at more than the sum of its parts and the quality of outcomes are, at times, compromised.

While a mean score of 6.73 suggest teams flounder more than they flourish, most teams, for some of the time, function as a cohesive entity. They are willing to work towards reaching consensus on matters of mutual interest and they seek agreement on matters important to the team's overall objectives.

2. Highest scoring discipline: DISCOVER (our mandate) at 7.02

This score suggests that teams feel they understand what their stakeholders expect and require of them, and that with which they have been commissioned. It also indicates a level of awareness of what stakeholders not only appreciate about the team but also what they look to the team to improve upon so things can be done more effectively to consistently deliver to their expectations.

This score suggests stakeholders and team members recognise they have the complementary skills to achieve the mandate.

3. Lowest scoring discipline: DELIVER (our results) at 6.57

Given that the predominant operating style is competitive, the quality and effectiveness of the results are, more often, compromised. Herein lies the greatest paradox. Teams exist to achieve what is only possible by working interdependently yet this is often the source of tension and frustration experienced by so many teams. Time and effort are wasted by not leveraging the collective capacity and capability inherent in a team.

This score suggests that team members devote most of their time and attention to achieving individual objectives rather than the team's (collective) performance goals. This is likely to remain the case until team accomplishments are recognised and rewarded at least equally to individual accomplishments as explained in point 4 below.

4. Lowest scoring indicator at 6.02

The lowest scoring indicator is 'Achieving the team's goals is recognised and rewarded above achieving individual goals (DELIVER).' The more individuals on a team who believe and experience being rewarded for their own individual efforts, the more teams are likely to perpetuate a competitive operating style and, therefore, will fail to unlock the collective capacity and capability to achieve what only teams can.

While 'rewards' are not the primary reason people join teams, how team members are rewarded has a significant influence on what they focus their individual and collective attention and energy on.

5. Highest scoring indicator at 7.86

The highest scoring indicator is 'The outcomes achieved are better than any individual could arrive at by themselves (DELIVER)'. This raises a question: Given that most team members believe the collective outcomes are so much better than what they could achieve alone, why do they focus most of their time and attention on delivering their own objectives and KPIs? The answer may simply be because that is what they are recognised and rewarded for.

6. Greatest indicator score variance at 3.17

The greatest variance occurs in 'The team behaviours and shared 'ways of working' have been identified and are consistently upheld (DESIGN)'. The variance represents the indicator in which respondents' scores varied the most. The score of 3.17 represents the average range between the respondent's highest and lowest score.

How team members relate and engage profoundly affects their ability to coordinate action and secure each other's commitment and cooperation to achieve what is most important.

7. Top-5 indicator scores

Indicator	Score	Discipline
The outcomes achieved are better than any individual could arrive at by themselves.	7.86	DELIVER
The team has been selected to have the complementary skills to achieve its mandate.	7.50	DISCOVER
Team members support each other and are committed to each other's ongoing learning and development.	7.31	DEVELOP
Team members are equally accountable for their own areas of responsibility and the team's collective goals.	6.95	DESIGN
Team members keep challenging themselves and others to keep developing and adding greater value.	6.91	DEVELOP

The top-5 indicators are distributed across four of the 5 Disciplines. This reinforces the significance of each discipline to the overall effectiveness of a team. It is relevant to note that two of the top-5 indicators relate to the 5th discipline (DEVELOP). One of the most distinguishing attributes of an effective team is the responsibility each team member takes for their own and others' learning, growth and success. Teams who create a culture of learning and are open to changing their beliefs are more effective in dealing with uncertainty, complexity and change.

8. Bottom-5 indicator scores

Indicator	Score	Discipline
Achieving the team's goals is recognised and rewarded above achieving individual goals.	6.02	DELIVER
The team behaviours and shared 'ways of working' have been identified and are consistently upheld.	6.03	DESIGN
Team members engage employees at all levels as transformational leaders.	6.14	DELIVER
Team members are open to receiving and giving feedback to each other on their performance and behaviours.	6.22	DEVELOP
The team has clear collective performance goals and success criteria that can only be achieved by working interdependently.	6.44	DELIVER

What teams aspire to be

During the discovery phase, individuals are asked to indicate the team operating style to which they aspire and to which they commit to achieving. For any team coaching program to be of value, it is essential that team members share a common vision of what success looks like and, more importantly, that they hold themselves and each other accountable to achieving the agreed end in mind.

Teams Operating Style – What teams aspire to

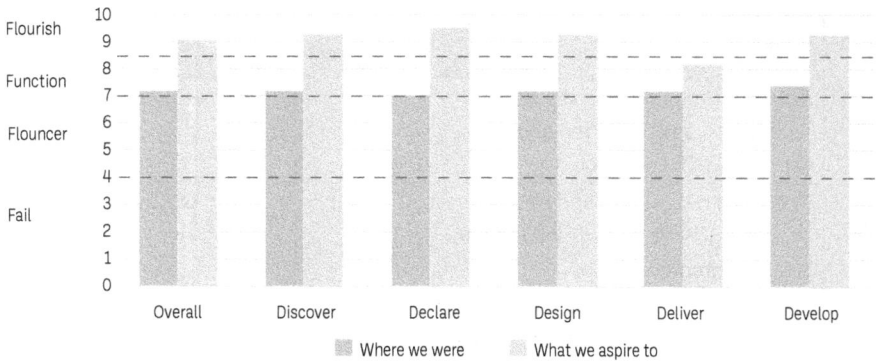

Legend: Where we were | What we aspire to

Y-axis categories: Flourish, Function, Flouncer, Fail (scale 0–10)

X-axis categories: Overall, Discover, Declare, Design, Deliver, Develop

The data here represents the operating style teams aspire to adopt. It is summarised into five key findings:

1. Teams aspire to adopt a collaborative operating style

The mean score of 9.3 indicates that teams both aspire to and accept they have the potential to operate in a collaborative style. While one would expect teams to aspire to adopt a collaborative operating style, it is more important to delve into how team members assessed the relative importance among the indicators.

2. Purpose (DECLARE) matters most at 9.80

Team members believe that identifying a unifying purpose that each team member understands and can articulate and demonstrate is most significant for transitioning to a collaborative, high performing and effective team. Central to any effective team is clarifying the unifying purpose and understanding the causes the team serves that are greater than itself.

As Mike Salisbury, CEO of McMillan Shakespeare Group shared, 'Coming to identify the executive team's purpose as "We unlock possibilities" has served to bring and focus our collective capability to achieve our 2020 strategy and beyond.' Purpose precedes profit.

3. Delivery is a consequence of, not the reason for, being a collaborative team

Analysis of what team members rated the top-5 most important indicators suggest that team members trust having a clear mandate, a unifying purpose, agreed ways of working and prerequisites for achieving and delivering the team's collective performance goals.

How important is it for the team to relate well to all its key stakeholders and for the team members to represent the whole team?	9.30	DISCOVER
How important is it for the team to have a clear commission and mandate from its stakeholders and those it reports to?	9.35	DISCOVER
How important is it for team members to know and consistently uphold the team's values?	9.38	DECLARE
How important is it for the team members to secure cooperation and commitment from each other?	9.46	DESIGN
How important is it for team members to understand, articulate and be committed to the team's purpose?	9.51	DECLARE

4. The least important among the most important

It's interesting to note that among what team members ranked as the five least important of the most important indicators all related to the Discipline to Deliver. Not that they believe delivery is unimportant, but that delivery is a consequence of embedding the four enabling disciplines: Discover, Declare, Design and Develop.

How important is it for the team to have clear performance goals that can only be achieved by working interdependently?	8.62	DELIVER
How important is it for achieving the team's goals to be recognised and rewarded above achieving individual goals?	8.67	DELIVER
How important is it for team members to engage employees at all levels as transformational leaders?	9.00	DELIVER
How important is it for the team to scan its stakeholders' environment and constantly attend to changing needs and perceptions?	9.00	DELIVER
How important is it for the team to have clear collective performance goals and success criteria that can only be achieved by working interdependently.	9.05	DELIVER

5. Lowest rated indicator among the most important

There may appear to be a paradox because the lowest scored indicator among the five most important relates to the importance of clarifying the team's collective performance goals. A rating of 8.62 falls within the collaborative range; however, team members feel it's important to bring perspective and balance when allocating their time, effort and action between achieving their individual KPIs and the team's collective performance goals.

The data reinforces that unless teams first focus on establishing an environment that they all want to be part of and that is aligned to the conditions for success, teams are unlikely to achieve and realise their collective capacity and capability. At best, they perform as a group while calling themselves a team.

DATA ANALYSIS FOR #1: DISCIPLINE TO DISCOVER

The first discipline team members assess as part of the *5 Disciplines of High Performing Teams Assessment* is Discover. The analysis of the responses shows the following:

Question	Team score	Importance indicator
The team has been selected to have the necessary complementary skills to achieve its mandate.	7.50	9.22* (rated 9th most important indicator)
The team has a clear mandate from its stakeholders.	6.88	9.35* (rated 4th most important indicator)
The team relates well to all its key stakeholders with the team members representing the whole team.	6.69	9.30* (rated 5th most important indicator)

While the Discipline to Discover scored highest at 7.02, two of the three indicators rated below the 70th percentile, which would suggest they warrant attention and focus.

It is nonetheless encouraging to see the importance teams have placed on securing greater understanding of their stakeholders' mandate and the opportunities this presents for becoming a more collaborative team, adding more value and having a greater impact.

A showcase of what's possible

When working with a corporate finance leadership team of a publicly listed organisation, I arranged for three stakeholders representing different interest groups to attend a workshop and share their experiences of working with the leadership team. At the CFOs request, we agreed not to inform other members of the team as he didn't want anyone lobbying for support and favourable positioning from their stakeholders.

Here is a summary of what was discussed in the workshop:

Question 1: What do you appreciate most about your relationship with the corporate finance leadership team?

1. The team's ability to respond to requests in a timely manner.
2. The improved efficiencies of the new purchase order system.
3. The 'partnership' approaches the team has adopted to working more collaboratively with internal stakeholder groups, for example, operations, compliance and IT.
4. The team's technical expertise and commercial acumen.
5. Greater openness made it possible for others to raise their concerns.

You cannot underestimate the significance of hearing what stakeholders appreciate about their relationship with the team. It recognises and reinforces the effort the team has made to improve their relationship with their stakeholders. Most importantly, it provides energy and motivation for the team to take the next step to add even greater value across the organisation.

Question 2: What do you find most difficult in your relationship with the corporate finance leadership team?

1. Omission of data provided, which results in increased levels of reactiveness and rework. A wasted collective effort.

2. Lack of flexibility in certain processes makes it difficult to respond to customer's requests.

3. Not having one point of contact to raise and escalate concerns results in multiple conversations and delayed resolutions.

4. Corporate finance not being proactively involved in providing guidance and advice on key processes like budgeting.

5. Lack of awareness and understanding of the corporate finance strategy and how it supports the overall business.

Knowing the stakeholders' concerns, the team can embrace opportunities to effect change and improve its service offering.

Question 3: In what ways do you want the corporate finance leadership team to step up to best meet your current and future needs?

1. To build on developing greater partnerships with the different business units across the organisation.

2. To engage with business units from the outset to secure understanding and buy-in to key change initiatives.

3. To educate the business about what and how corporate finance could add greater value to other business units.

4. Identify agreed ways of working that would establish more effective working relationships between corporate finance and its stakeholders.

5. Provide more information and less data to help business leaders make more informed decisions. As one stakeholder offered, 'Provide more insights and trends rather than reports and data.'

Stepping up

Having collected and considered the stakeholder feedback, the corporate finance leadership team and the stakeholders co-created a revised mandate that presented a clearer understanding of and commitment to deliver on the original mandate. The team resolved to deliver on:

- Our IMPERATIVES (to add greater value and have greater impact). Corporate finance will:

    - Be a business partner, not a service function.

    - Drive joint accountability and ownership, not simply report outcomes.

    - Not just start the conversation but be part of the solution.

    - Elevate processing to reporting and analysis.

    - Elevate reporting numbers to identifying business drivers.

- Shift from a historical focus to identifying trends and patterns to enable greater dynamic forecasting.

- Our COMMITMENTS (to achieve our 'customer mandate', deliver on our 'imperatives' and step up to what our customers require).

To be a business partner with our customers, we will:

- Move beyond intent to 'being a partner'.

- Proactively engage with our customers to provide valued and needed advice, guidance and help with finance, risk and compliance matters.

- Engage with the business from the outset / onset of a business challenge and opportunity. Set up joint working committees on key initiatives to drive the 'transformational agenda'.

- Know our key stakeholders and agree on the common objectives and ways of working together. Clarify roles and responsibilities and agree on timelines of expected outcomes / deliverables.

- Be honest, give feedback, not store up issues and have more honest conversations.

Tell our 'story' and educate our stakeholders:

- Proactively share what we do, what we're working on, and what we've done that has been valued and is of benefit to our stakeholders.

- Identify what knowledge and skill gaps our customers have and how we can address each. For example:

  - Explain why certain items are allocated to certain cost centres.

  - Provide insight into how to 'move forward' and not focus on 'explaining the past'.

  - Improve budget reporting. Work together on a common understanding of a 'number'.

  - Identify how and where to access information to explain the numbers.

  - Present information in a way that's easier to understand and relevant to making more informed decisions.

  - Identify and share insights and trends. Identify the 'trends as friends' and the 'trends as enemies'.

Provide the tools and processes:

- Help our customers make better decisions and take wiser action.

- Identify and implement tools to deliver reports and information business leaders require.

- Better analyse the business, and identify patterns and trends.

The Discipline to Discover the mandate with which a team has been commissioned is fundamental to becoming a collaborative, high performing team. Most important is the commitment the team makes to consistently reviewing and revising the mandate in order to ensure alignment on what the team is focused on accomplishing together.

Reflection

To make a start, I invite your team to reflect on the following questions and share the answers with your stakeholders. Compare your insights with your stakeholders' perspectives and identify the similarities and differences. Then discuss and agree to further understanding the mandate.

1.   What do they appreciate most about their relationship with the leadership team?

2.   What do they find most difficult about their relationship with the leadership team?

3.   How do they want the leadership team to step up and change to best meet their mandate?

To uphold and maintain the Discipline to Discover as a team, commit to reflecting annually on the following and test the team's insights with the different stakeholder groups:

1.   How may the stakeholders' mandate have changed?

2.   What is now most important for us to adapt and adjust in order to meet our stakeholders' expectations?

DATA ANALYSIS FOR #2: DISCIPLINE TO DECLARE

Here is a summary of the scores from the *5 Disciplines of High Performing Teams Assessment* data:

Question	Team score	Importance indicator
Team members understand, can articulate and are commitment to the team's purpose.	6.55	9.51* (rated the most important indicator)
Team members know and consistently uphold the team's values.	6.64	9.38* (rated 3rd most important indicator)

While the team members' current level of understanding, ability to articulate and commitment to the team's purpose is ranked the 8th lowest score of the 18 team assessment indicators, there is unanimity across the teams that bringing clarity to the team purpose is the most important factor to becoming a collaborative, high performing team.

As one CEO shared, 'Our executive team's purpose needs more discussion and buy-in. Our individual values are clear every time we meet but I suspect we need more discussion about what the executive team values need to be. By this, I mean the executive team's values, not the organisation's values.'

To remain committed to the team's purpose is the most distinguishing attribute of collaborative, high performing teams.

The difference purpose makes

When working with the senior leadership team (SLT) of a division in a large government organisation, it was evident that the lack of clarity on its purpose was a source of much confusion and frustration, and a contributor to a level of dysfunctional interpersonal working relationships within the division.

A summary of the team's initial *5 Disciplines of High Performing Teams Assessment* revealed that the team, when at its best, adopted a competitive team operating style but for much of the time operated in a combative style. The team's overall score of 4.3 substantiates this claim.

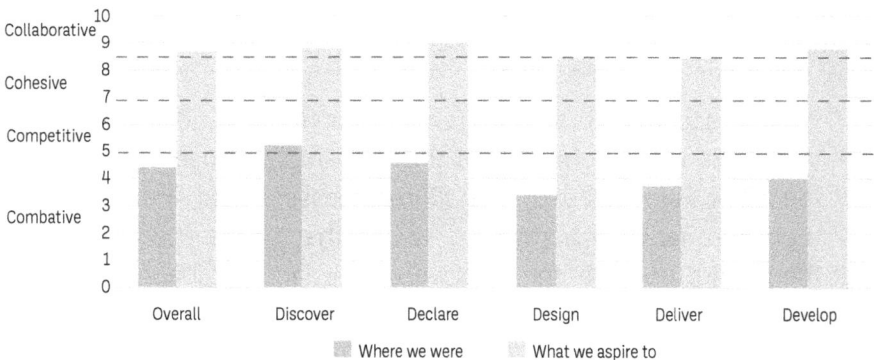

The extended leadership team (ELT), most of whom individually were accountable to an SLT member, was purportedly responsible for implementing key initiatives and projects the SLT sponsored. As a consequence of neither the SLT nor ELT having a clear purpose, considerable time and effort were wasted in duplicated effort because of unclear lines of accountability and responsibility.

Following a facilitated process, the SLT and ELT respectively agreed to their purpose:

- SLT: *We lead the way to new possibilities.*
- ELT: *Together we create the way for tomorrow.*

The distinction between the SLT 'leading' and the ELT 'creating' has enabled both teams to better coordinate action and to fill their respective responsibilities more effectively. As one ELT member shared, 'The SLT also becomes more effective to disseminate decisions made or policies changed to the ELT and other team members. They have opened channels for team members to escalate any operational issue because of proposed policy change.'

Reflection

In the ever-changing and dynamic world we have come to live in, it's critical that teams review and revise their purpose to ensure they remain relevant to their stakeholders and aligned in their collective endeavours.

As a team, commit to annually reflecting on the following questions and share insights:

1. For what sake do we exist as a team?
2. What cause, greater than ourselves, is now more important for us to serve?
3. How will this differ from our current purpose? Declare it.

DATA ANALYSIS FOR #3: DISCIPLINE TO DESIGN

How effective are your working relationships?

Let's look at the data and what teams feel about the quality of their working relationships. In Part Five, I will address how the quality of conversations is fundamental to developing effective working relationships, particularly in relation to discussing the undiscussables.

In respect to the Discipline to Design, here is a summary of the scores from the *5 Disciplines of High Performing Teams Assessment:*

Question	Team score	Importance indicator
The team behaviours and shared 'ways of working' have been identified and are consistently upheld.	6.03	9.20* (2nd lowest scored indicator)
Team members secure cooperation and commitment from each other.	6.88	9.46* (2nd most important indicator)
Team members are equally accountable for their own areas of responsibility and the team's collective goals.	6.95	9.28
All team members are engaged and involved, and the team uses its diversity.	6.69	9.28

An overall score of 6.64 for the Discipline to Design supports the view shared by team members that between 30% and 50%

of the time, teams do not perform at their best and operate at less than the sum of their parts for more of the time. The more common contributing patterns of behaviour shared by team members include:

- When team members feel unable to effect change beyond their own area of responsibility, they default into a siloed mentality in thought and action.

- Where team members fail to recognise and understand their interdependencies and the impact their actions have on others.

- When team members react defensively to others' questions and challenges and fail to access the value in diversity of thinking.

- When team members fail to hold each other accountable to agreed commitments and not call out undesired attitudes and behaviours.

- When team members avoid engaging in what are deemed to be 'difficult conversations' for fear of the consequences of disagreeing or conflicting with others.

- When team members are misaligned to the performance goals most important to team priorities.

Unsurprisingly, team members believe the second most important indicator, following the need to have a unifying team purpose, is the need to secure greater cooperation and commitment from each other. Teams rise and fall based on the quality of their working relationships.

What it takes to build effective relationships

Relationships happen in conversation. How team members relate and engage when together and apart happens in and from the quality of their conversations. Nothing changes until something changes. The starting point to shifting the quality of the team's working relationship is the commitment to reflect and observe the dynamic—how each person feels about being part of the team. This requires creating a safe and supportive space to share. To make a start, invite each team member to reflect on and share their insights to the following questions about their current working relationships:

1. Which relationships in the team are most important?

2. How would you characterise your relationship with this / these person(s)?

3. What aspects of the relationship work well for you?

4. What do you value about this relationship?

5. What areas of concern do you have about this relationship?

6. How may you be contributing to your concerns about the relationship?

7. What can be done to address your concerns?

8. What do you commit to change to improve the relationship?

Then be vulnerable and demonstrate your courage by sharing and engaging in a conversation to build the relationship.

The impact relationships can have

An analysis of a team's scores to the Discipline to Design revealed the following:

From a comparison of the team's score in each of the 5 Disciplines, the Discipline to Design was the lowest score at 3.3. This score characterised the interpersonal dynamic within the team as typically competitive and more often combative. Low trust, indifference and disrespect of others' views and opinions were a common experience among team members.

Further analysis of the scores associated with the Discipline to Design showed the following:

Question	Team score	Importance indicator
The team behaviours and shared 'ways of working' have been identified and are consistently upheld.	1.6* (lowest recorded indicator score)	8.0
Team members secure cooperation and commitment from each other.	5.0	9.0
Team members are mutually accountable for their own areas of responsibility and the team's collective goals.	4.4	8.6
All team members are engaged and involved, and the team uses its diversity.	2.4	8.4

Understandably, the team prioritised putting in place agreed ways of working to ensure its working relationship improved to enable them to better coordinate action to achieve their goals.

Following a reflective and facilitated process, the team identified and committed to the following agreed ways of working:

1. We encourage each other to share. We offer our perspectives and show respect, despite how similar or different others' perspectives are to our own.

2. We are vulnerable with each other and share our fears and concerns.

3. We call out when others break our trust and deal with the situation in a respectful manner.

4. We make important and informed decisions together and honour the decisions made unless we collectively change any decision.

5. We hold ourselves and each other accountable and accept responsibility for our actions and commitments.

6. We share learning from both our collective wins and failings.

7. We deal with conflicts and disagreements as they arise and work towards reaching an acceptable outcome.

8. We make it safe to discuss difficult topics between and among ourselves in an open and trusting manner and without fear.

Most encouraging was that 12 months later, following a reassessment of the *5 Disciplines of High Performing Teams Assessment*, the team's Discipline to Design scores improved 100% from 3.3 to 6.6. This improvement was endorsed by what some of the team members across the organisation had to say about what they felt had changed in how the team teamed better together. Here are some of the comments they shared:

- 'One obvious change is that team members are more personable. They listen and attend to our pain points and shared their experiences during COVID-19.'

- 'The team is more willing to listen to our feedback and options without judging. We feel far more relaxed and worry less about being judged when sharing ideas.'

- 'The team is more effective in how it disseminates decisions made to other team members. It also opened up channels for team members to escalate any operational issues because of proposed policy change. This became obvious during COVID-19 when lots of quick decisions were being made for staff benefits and reimbursements.'

Relationships are the lifeblood of any team. While we appreciate that we see and do things differently to one another, teams who invest time and effort in building quality working relationships will always outperform teams who do not.

Teams built on quality and effective working relationships care deeply for everyone within the team. They trust one another. They feel safe and are able to be direct with one another. Challenging one another serves to bring clarity rather than a feeling of being pushed aside.

In high trust and flourishing teams, conflict serves to access different views rather than leave others feeling shut down. Criticism is a rich source of learning rather than a tool to weaken others.

Reflection

To build and maintain the quality of the team's working relationships, commit to regularly reflecting on and sharing insights on the following:

1. What may team members be saying or doing that may be hindering the effectiveness of the working relationships?

2. What is most important for team members to commit to changing in order to better relate and engage together to achieve the greatest possible outcomes?

DATA ANALYSIS FOR #4: DISCIPLINE TO DELIVER

Groups become collaborative, high performing teams through disciplined action and an unwavering commitment to the 5 Disciplines. Let's look at what the data from the *5 Disciplines of High Performing Teams Assessment* revealed with respect to the Discipline to Deliver.

Question	Team score	Importance indicator
The outcomes achieved are better than any individual could arrive at by themselves	7.86 (Highest scored indicator)	9.05
The team has clear collective performance goals and success criteria that can only be achieved by working interdependently.	6.44* (5th lowest scored indicator)	8.62
Achieving the team's goals is recognised and rewarded above achieving individual goals.	6.02* (lowest scored indicator)	8.67
Team members leave meetings feeling more focused, supported and energised.	6.50	9.28
The team scans its stakeholders' environment and constantly attends to changing needs and perceptions.	6.48	9.00
Team members engage employees at all levels as transformational leaders.	6.14* (3rd lowest scored indicator)	9.00

Teams exist to achieve what no other entity can. That said, for teams to access their collective capacity and capability, team members are required to understand, own and accept accountability for the team's collective goals.

Reflecting on the above scores, it's little surprise that when team members are asked to articulate the team's collective goals, there is greater *misalignment* than *alignment*. Furthermore, given individual goals are recognised and rewarded above the team's collective goals, it's no wonder team members focus mostly on their individual responsibilities and less on their collective accountabilities.

Of greater concern, as indicated by the score 6.50 to question 4 above, is the time and energy team members waste in inefficient and unproductive meetings.

Leaders I work with, on average, claim to spend 60% of their time and energy in meetings. More concerning is their claim that 50% of these meetings are ineffective.

Imagine the direct and indirect costs of wasting 15 hours a week in ineffective meetings. It's no wonder levels of stress and burnout are as high as they are.

Flourishing, high performing teams make meetings matter because:

1. They know the purpose of and the agenda for each meeting.
2. They know what outcomes are sought from the meeting.
3. Most important, they come prepared to contribute.

Floundering teams, on the other hand, meet for the sake of it:

1. They show up to meetings confused about why, what and who.

2. They spend half the time deliberating about the agenda.

3. They leave the meeting feeling frustrated and demoralised by inaction.

Reflection

Here are 10 strategies to help teams more effectively coordinate action and secure greater cooperation and commitment to get done what is most important.

1. Start with the quality of working relationships

To improve the quality of results, first improve the quality of working relationships. A lack of trust or mutual respect, or anything that reduces the capacity to maintain working relationships, will result in wasted time, effort, costs and disruption.

2. Begin with the end in mind

Before making a request of another person, craft a vision of what success looks like. What does 'done' look like? What are the conditions of satisfactory completion? Once the end in mind is clear, share it with those with whom you intend to coordinate action. Everything is created twice: first in one's own mind then in the understanding of others.

3. Understand the distinction between making and managing a commitment

To coordinate action and get something done requires us to engage in the conversations relevant to making and managing commitments. There are four interdependent stages, each requiring a different conversation before we can effectively coordinate action:

a. Conversations for Clarity is about making a clear and effective request of another person.

b. Conversations for Commitment is about seeking a trusted commitment from the other person looked upon to deliver an outcome.

c. Conversations for Accountability is about managing expectations and declaring satisfactory completeness.

d. Conversations for Appreciation is about acknowledging the other person for meeting the conditions of satisfactory delivery.

4. Stage 1: Master the art of making effective requests

This is about being a 'responsible customer' by making it as easy as possible for the 'performer' to know what they are expected to do. Be clear about the scope of work, specify the required outcomes / deliverables, and provide clarity on expected timelines and the conditions of satisfaction. Most importantly, test the performer's understanding of the requests and identify any concerns they may have before committing.

5. Stage 2: Seek a clear and trusted commitment

The Conversations for Commitment is where the performer takes responsibility to make it clear if they are making a definite commitment or not.

Where a request is combined with an acceptance, a commitment (i.e. promise) is made. This stage is fraught with a risk of misunderstanding and miscommunication. It is the performer's responsibility to not give a 'slippery commitment' based on an assumed understanding or an unspoken concern they may have with the request.

6. Stage 3: Be jointly accountable for managing the commitment

Respectfully hold people accountable for what they have explicitly committed to do but may not have fulfilled. The spirit of this conversation is not about blaming or getting back at others; it is about respecting the commitment. As the 'requester', take responsibility to inform the performer if the request is no longer important or if the time frame for completion has altered. Circumstances change; therefore, as the performer, you must inform the requester in the event the request cannot be fulfilled according to what was agreed.

7. Stage 4: Evaluate the fulfilment of the commitment

In the event the commitment has been fulfilled, acknowledge, recognise and express appreciation. The two most important words in the Conversations for Appreciation are 'thank you'. In the event the commitment has not been satisfactorily met, re-engage the Conversations for Accountability.

8. Be mindful of untested expectations

In the busyness to get things done, be mindful of what commitments and promises one may have listened to that the other person never made. Be alert to one's untested expectations.

9. Ask, 'How may I have contributed?'

If we are honest with ourselves, we tend to blame others for not delivering on what was requested of them. We may even go further and accuse them of having a lack of accountability. We seldom look to ourselves and ask, 'How may I have contributed to the request not being met?' There is always the possibility you could have made a sloppy request.

10. Sloppy request, slippery commitment

A sloppy request will always get a slippery commitment. Just because you have a clear idea of what needs to get done does not mean the person you are asking shares the same level of understanding and clarity. Performance, productivity and relationships are closely bound up with how effectively we make and manage commitments. It is worth the effort.

DATA ANALYSIS FOR #5: DISCIPLINE TO DEVELOP

How effectively do teams learn?

Teams are living, evolving and dynamic systems that are always having to adapt and adjust to deal with the inherent uncertainty and unpredictability. This requires teams to learn. To be a high performing team requires a commitment from all members to be open to learning with and from each other.

Let's look at the data from the *5 Disciplines of High Performing Teams Assessment* with regard to the Discipline to Develop:

Question	Team score	Importance indicator
Team members are open to receiving and giving feedback to each other on their performance and behaviours.	6.22* (4th lowest scored indicator)	9.23
Team members support each other and are committed to each other's ongoing learning and development.	7.31* (3rd highest scored indicator)	9.11
Team members keep challenging themselves and others to keep developing and adding greater value.	6.91	9.12

The following key themes and indicators are worth noting:

- The paradox. While team members express their support and commitment to each other's ongoing learning and development (3rd highest scored indicator), they are less open to giving and receiving feedback from one another (question 1 above ranked as 4th lowest scored indicator).

- The second lowest score indicated (relating to the Discipline to Design) is team behaviours and shared ways of working have been identified and are consistently upheld. This suggests that 'learning' is not embedded as an agreed way of working. Consequently, team members may not feel safe and may lack the trust and confidence needed to provide feedback to others. This would be especially so if they anticipated others would react defensively to perceived criticism.

- In his book, *Drive*, Daniel Pink discusses the results of extensive global research regarding human behaviour across different cultures and socio-economic groups in first, second and third world countries. It was found that despite our differences, we are intrinsically motivated by three common drivers: purpose, mastery and autonomy. Mastery is the opportunity to learn, grow and apply skills to best affect our work and is consistent with the responses to question 3 above.

> To learn is to observe. We can't change what we can't see.

Reflection

To develop the team's collective wisdom and to support each team member's learning and success, commit to always asking yourself:

1. What did we do that enabled us to succeed?

2. What did we do or not do that contributed to us failing to achieve our desired outcome?

3. What did I learn today that will help me and the team tomorrow? Then share it.

COMING UP IN PART FIVE

Being a smart high performing team requires the uncompromising commitment from each team member to uphold the 5 Disciplines whether teaming together or apart. Above all else, teams rise and fall based on the quality of their working relationships. Relationships happen through conversations. What is said, how it's said and how it's listened to are fundamental to how team members develop greater levels of understanding. This makes for more informed decisions and greater cooperation and commitment to get done what needs to be done. Let's turn our attention to how teams create the space for all to feel safe to speak their truth and ensure nothing is undiscussable.

Part Five
Making it happen

Discussing the undiscussables

*'People almost never change
without first feeling understood.'*
—Douglas Stone

The quality of team members' working relationships is how they access their collective capacity and capability. Relationships happen in conversation. Teams operate in conversation and results happen through conversation. In this section, I will share how teams can radically shift the quality of their conversations so that they are able to operate at more than the sum of their parts and coordinate action to achieve the greatest outcomes.

Conversations are the lifeblood of effective working relationships. Leaders and team members continuously interact with one another through conversation. Their conversational proficiency determines the levels of trust and commitment required to implement strategies, systems and processes to achieve desired results.

What is and is not said in conversations, how it is (or is not) said and how it is (or is not) listened to is crucial to how efficiently and effectively leaders, teams and team members perform. Conversations that do not generate new insights, innovative practices, effective actions and positive results are unproductive; they create and perpetuate costly communication breakdowns and generate waste.

HOW EFFECTIVELY DO WE DISCUSS THE UNDISCUSSABLES?

It often feels too hard to have the difficult conversations; we avoid them in the hope that they will resolve themselves. It can seem difficult to speak one's truth when giving someone feedback or addressing a difference of opinion. Flourishing teams distinguish themselves by being spoken about rather than being unspoken. Floundering teams are more unspoken than they are spoken about.

		STATE	▶ BEHAVIOUR	▶ IMPACT
🔊	SPOKEN	Safe	Truthful	Connected
		Secure	Sincere	Clarity
💭	UNSPOKEN	Caution	Insincere	Confusion
		Fear	Censored	Closed

In today's 'always on', fast-paced environment, leaders increasingly feel like they operate in permanent white water, facing increasing complexity, uncertainty and rapid change. In such circumstances, working relationships deteriorate and leaders remain stuck in recurring, limiting behavioural patterns that produce suboptimal results.

It's not surprising then that research conducted by Perlow, Hadley and Eun showed 71% of leaders claim meetings are unproductive and inefficient, and 62% of leaders claim that meetings miss the opportunity to bring the team closer together. The consequences of not speaking one's truth or believing it is futile to question or share differing perspectives leaves people feeling disengaged and disempowered.

Team members need to share more of their truth (together) to understand complex situations, consider options and make more informed choices. The effectiveness of their actions depends on the effectiveness of their working relationships and the quality of their conversations on crucial issues. William Ury, author of *Getting to Yes*, says, 'We must create an environment where even the most serious disputes are handled not based on coercion or force, but from mutual respect and coexistence. Far from eliminating differences, our challenge is to make the workplace safe for differences.'

THE FOUR ELEMENTS OF EVERY CONVERSATION

It's important to appreciate the interdependence between the four elements of a conversation if we are to understand why we get stuck in difficult conversations.

Four elements of all conversations...

First is **speaking**. This is what we say when in conversation with others. When speaking, we have access to the '6 speech acts' as described by philosopher, John Searle:

1. Assessments are our opinions and judgements: *What a beautiful painting*.

2. Assertions are what we use to describe what is and is not factual in our world: what we know to be true: *The painting was painted by Van Gogh*.

3. Declarations are statements made with an authority that brings about a change in circumstances and the generation of a different reality: *At 2.00 pm today, I'm handing in my resignation*.

4. Requests are attempts to have people do things for us: *Could you please review the document and check it for spelling and grammatical errors?*

5. Offers are when we put ourselves forward to do things for others: *Would you like me to make you a cup of tea?*

6. Promises are when we commit ourselves to doing things for others: *I will send you the final draft by 4.00 pm tomorrow*.

Articulating what we do is significant because we speak from our concerns. We are never not 'in concern'. We speak from what is important to us and from what is not going as well as we would like.

Second is **listening**. The greatest gift we can give to another is to leave them feeling listened to. To listen to another is to understand the other. More important than listening with the intent to agree is to commit to understanding what the other means. By listening, we make meaning of what the other person is saying. There are two crucial elements to how we listen. The first is how effective we are at listening to what the other person means by what they are saying. Most of the time we listen with the intention of responding rather than understanding; therefore, it's not surprising that we get stuck having difficult conversations. The hidden element in listening is recognising where we are listening *from*. As we speak to our concerns, we listen from our concerns.

Let's assume that a colleague whom you distrust walks past you in the corridor. They say, 'Well done, Joe. Your presentation this morning was brilliant.' Because you are listening from your concern about not trusting them, your inward response is *yeah right, how insincere*. To be an effective listener is one of the hardest and most powerful skills to master.

Third is **mood**. As emotional beings, we are never not 'in mood'. Moods are predispositions for action: everything we say and do is because of the mood we're in at the time. Let's go back to the example of the distrusting colleague. Your assessment of their untrustworthiness evoked an irritated and intolerant mood, which predisposed you to dismiss and question the sincerity of their comment.

Fourth is **body**. Our mood, and how we speak and listen, happens 'in body'. Our physiology reflects our embodied moods. Think of a time that your mood caused you to feel tension in your body. How did this affect your speaking and listening? We live 'in body'; therefore, our bodies are a manifestation of our mood and how we speak and listen.

What makes conversations difficult?

As William Shakespeare once said, 'There is nothing either good or bad but thinking makes it so.' Don't we all wish this to be true of those difficult conversations we need to have but mostly avoid?

How much time—on any working day—do you spend in conversation? Think about the amount of time spent in team meetings, telephone conversations, 1:1 meetings, emails and voicemails. Next consider what percentage of those conversations are effective. An effective conversation has these elements:

1. What is important be shared is shared.
2. What is said and how it is understood is aligned.
3. The desired outcome is achieved.

Over the past 15 years, I've asked leaders and team members those two questions. The most consistent responses are they spend between 60% and 80% of their time in conversation, while only 40% to 60% of their conversations are deemed effective. Think about the consequences of only 40%–60% of your conversations being effective. Think about how much wasted time and effort is expended. Our current state of overwhelming busyness and the consequent lack of ability to discern what's most and least important is a result of the amount of time spent in unproductive and ineffective conversations.

To understand why we get stuck in difficult conversations, it's important to appreciate the 'operating pathway' to which we are biologically predisposed as humans. By 'operating pathway' I refer to the sequence and interdependence between our thoughts, moods, actions and consequences.

Every conversation has a set of assumptions, beliefs and opinions. These thoughts elicit moods, which predispose us to actions and lead us to consequences. They are desired and intentional or undesired and unintentional.

Our operating pathway

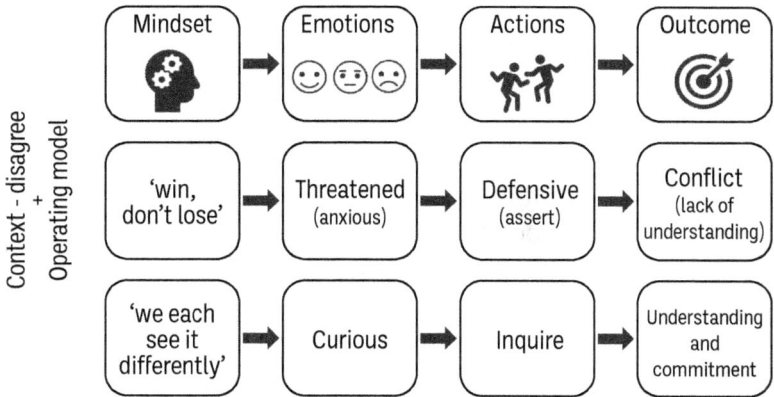

Let me demonstrate with a practical example. Assume you agreed to converse with a colleague to resolve an important matter you both strongly disagree on.

Every conversation has a context (the purpose for having the conversation) and a construct (the operating model / style each party adopts in the conversation). It all starts with your mindset—the beliefs, assumptions, opinions and perspectives you hold when you come into the conversation. Let's assume your mindset is that you must 'win' this argument. Believing you must win and not lose will trigger feelings of anxiety and worry. You'll be thinking *what will happen if I lose?*

In a mood of anxiety and worry, you are predisposed to defend and assert your viewpoint, believing you're right and the other person is wrong. It is less likely that you will reach a resolution and more likely that you will perpetuate misunderstanding and escalate the levels of tension and conflict.

> Difficult conversations are difficult because of how we think (our mindset).

However, if your mindset is *we each see this differently and have different views on how to resolve it*, the conversation and resolution would be quite the opposite. It is important to remember here that you can only control the mindset you show up with—there's nothing you can do directly to change the other person's mindset.

By accepting that each party perceives things differently, you are likely to elicit a mood of curiosity and wonder. By bringing a mood of curiosity, you are open to inquire and seek clarity about the other person's thinking. This will help you to better understand the differences, which is crucial for both parties to move closer to a co-created resolution.

Unilateral control vs mutual learning

As we know, there are no guarantees with human behaviour: we are unpredictable by nature. However, we get stuck in difficult conversations because we adopt what Roger Schwarz, author of *Smart Leaders, Smarter Teams*, calls a 'unilateral control' operating style. Difficult conversations can only be effectively resolved by adopting a 'mutual learning' operating style.

In distinguishing unilateral control from mutual learning, I'd like to acknowledge the work and contribution of the late Chris Argyris, Roger Schwarz and Fred Kofman in the field of study and practice.

It's important to acknowledge that both operating styles are relevant and applicable, albeit in different circumstances. To master effective conversations, it's crucial to know under what circumstances each operating style is most appropriate, and to declare and effectively demonstrate the style. For example, in crisis situations it may be more appropriate to declare a unilateral control approach and to ensure others are aware and understand why certain courses of action are being taken. When it's important to better understand others' perspectives and to secure greater cooperation and commitment from others, a unilateral control operating style would be counter-productive. Yet, not knowing others' experience of us, more often than we care to believe, would be more aligned to unilateral control. How we think we come across is more often not what others experience of us. Let me give you an example: How often have you been in a meeting when either you or someone else has 'respectfully' suggested to take the topic of discussion 'offline'? While I accept that sometimes it may be appropriate, in many cases it's because we fear 'losing' or embarrassing ourselves and feel it would be easier to exercise our power in a 1:1 rather than in a more public space with colleagues watching.

The respective mindsets, behaviours and associated consequences applicable to each operating style are best illustrated below:

Unilateral Control Mindset

Core Values and Assumptions	Strategies	Consequences
• To achieve my goals I need to get others t do what I know is right • I am right about what others need; if they disagree, they are wrong. • If there are any disagreements, win, don't lose. • I act rationally. • I understand the situation; if others see it differently, they do not. • I have pure motives; if others disagree it will be because they have impure motives. • My feelings are justified. • Errors and failuures are embarrassing and should be covered up.	• Advocate my position. • Minimise expressing negative thoughts or feelings. • Keep my reasoning private, and discourage enquiry into it. • Don't ask others about their reasoning. • Ask leading questions. • Ease in. • Tactically step back and temporarily concede control to others to avoid appearing controlling. • Save face.	• Misunderstanding. • Surface calm, but conflict can break out. • Likely stalemate underlying problems persist. • Mistrust and defensiveness on both sides. • Self sealing processes. • Limited learning on both sides. Reduced effectiveness of the relationship. • Decreased human quality of the relationship.

Mutual Learning Mindset

Core Values and Assumptions	Strategies	Consequences
• We need to find and use the most valid information. • We both need to make free and informed choices. • I act from internal commitment. • I have some information; others have other information. • Each of us may see things the other does not. • Differences are opportunities for learning. • Errors and failures are opportunities for learning. • We are both trying to act with integrity, given our respective situations.	• Test assumptions and inferences. • Share all relevant information. • Use specific examples and agree on the meanings of important words. • Explain reasoning and intent. • Focus on interests, not positions. • Combine advocacy and inquiry. • Jointly designed approach. • Discuss undiscussables.	• Increased understanding. • Reduced conflict and defensiveness. • Increase trust. • Fewer self-sealing processes. • Increased learning. • Increased effectiveness. • Enhanced human quality of the relationship.

A unilateral control operating style gets us stuck in difficult conversations because we show up believing we understand the situation and if others disagree it's because they don't understand it. We believe we are right and if others disagree, it's because they're wrong. We believe they have ulterior motives; therefore, our frustration and irritation with them is justifiable. We legitimately lay the blame on them.

When adopting a unilateral control operating style, others experience us as mostly stating our own views and not inquiring into theirs. We withhold information for fear of compromising or undermining our position. We speak in general terms, keep our reasoning private and don't ask others for their reasoning. We focus on protecting and defending our own position rather than mutual interests. We act on untested assumptions and inferences and do all we can to keep control of the conversation. Does this feel all too familiar? Remember, it's easier to recognise these behaviours in others than in ourselves.

How do others experience you?

To help you be a better observer of yourself, and to help you identify your predominant operating style, you can assess yourself against these indicators. Our mindset (our beliefs, perspectives, assumptions and opinions) impacts how we feel, how we behave and the results we achieve. Give thought to how you believe others would typically experience you against each of these 20 statements and rate yourself using the scale provided. For each statement, circle the appropriate score.

Indicators	Totally disagree	Disagree	Unsure	Agree	Totally agree
I am open to being influenced by others.	1	2	3	4	5
When I propose a solution, I inquire as to what others think of the idea.	1	2	3	4	5
I share relevant information and am transparent about my feelings, opinions and beliefs.	1	2	3	4	5

Indicators	Totally disagree	Disagree	Unsure	Agree	Totally agree
I adopt a win-win approach to dealing with disagreements.	1	2	3	4	5
I share information and give examples to explain and ensure others understand what I mean.	1	2	3	4	5
I am aware when I make assumptions and test whether my assumptions are correct before taking action.	1	2	3	4	5
I seek others' commitment to an action plan before proceeding.	1	2	3	4	5
I explain my reasoning when disagreeing with others.	1	2	3	4	5
I share information openly to ensure the most informed decisions are made.	1	2	3	4	5
I first clarify my thinking before making assumptions.	1	2	3	4	5
I seek feedback from others on how my thinking and behaviour may be contributing to the problem.	1	2	3	4	5
When working with others, I ensure important decisions are made together rather than deciding privately and unilaterally what to do.	1	2	3	4	5

Indicators	Totally disagree	Disagree	Unsure	Agree	Totally agree
I hold myself accountable for my actions and results.	1	2	3	4	5
When resolving difficult issues, I focus on identifying solutions that meet the parties' common interests rather than focusing on protecting my own.	1	2	3	4	5
I admit to how my actions may have contributed to the problem arising.	1	2	3	4	5
I explain my reasoning and intent when proposing an alternate viewpoint.	1	2	3	4	5
I accept others may see things differently and have different information, and I see 'diversity' as an opportunity rather than a threat.	1	2	3	4	5
I engage in rather than avoid the difficult conversations to resolve issues.	1	2	3	4	5
I generate solutions with the team's interests and needs in mind.	1	2	3	4	5
I am curious and seek to understand why others disagree with me before reacting.	1	2	3	4	5

To score yourself, simply add your scores for all 20 questions and indicate the score in the appropriate score range below.

Score: 2–50	I try to achieve my goals by controlling the situation. I try to get others to do what I want them to do while keeping myself minimally influenced by others. I make poor decisions that others are reluctant to implement because I'm not fully committed. As a consequence, I take longer to get things done, have strained relationships, appear defensive and experience higher levels of stress.
Score: 51–75	I am somewhat controlling and only occasionally open to being influenced by others. When I make decisions, others agree to implement the required action but do not always act with a real sense or level of commitment. As a consequence, when others disagree with me, I avoid addressing their differences, which leads to suboptimal results.
Score: 76–100	I make quality and more innovative decisions by creating a pool of accurate information and a shared understanding of the situation I face. I am curious about others' interests and jointly design solutions that address these. I can be trusted to follow through on my commitments. Because of high trust, I create a safe environment in which others learn with and from one another. As a result, I generate a motivated environment that others choose to be part of and commit to get things done. Others find it satisfying to work with me.

Reflect on your scores and identify what three behaviours you recognise are important to adapt and adopt in order to develop more of a mutual learning operating style and thereby facilitating more cohesive, collaborative and effective working relationships:

1.

2.

3.

Effective teams master a mutual
learning operating style.

IT'S ALL VERY WELL BUT ...

I'm often asked, 'What happens when I choose to show up with a mutual learning operating style and the other person operates from a unilateral control style?' This is reality and there is nothing we can do to directly change how others show up to a conversation. However, you can control your choice of operating style, so choose wisely. Choose one that provides the greatest possibility to share more information, to better understand others, to make more informed decisions and to take wiser action.

When we choose a mutual learning operating style, we access greater power with others rather than adopting a unilateral control operating style and competing to exercise power over others.

When adopting a mutual learning operating style, we accept that our assessments, beliefs and assumptions may be different to others. We see the world differently: not as it is but as we are. We have access to different information. Two people reading the same report may have very different interpretations of its essence and, therefore, propose different courses of action. So, who is right or wrong? Neither. Each is right in how they see things. We are the holders of *our* truth and not *the* truth. From a mutual learning operating style, we accept that we may disagree with others. We see disagreements as opportunities to learn rather than to sit in judgement of others' thinking and motives. Most importantly, we come with the openness to accept that we may be contributing to the problem in ways we don't see. This doesn't mean taking responsibility for it; it means being open to how others may feel we could be contributing.

By adopting a mutual learning mindset, we open ourselves to behaving in ways that foster greater understanding. We state our views and ask others to share their perspectives; we balance advocacy and inquiry. We share all the information: data, assumptions, beliefs and opinions. We use examples to make sure others know and understand what we mean. We explain our reasoning and intent in saying what we do. We focus on our mutual interests rather than on our personal position. We know and test our assumptions and inferences, and jointly design how we move forward together. In mutual learning, nothing is undiscussable.

THREE MUTUAL LEARNING FRAMEWORKS

To enable teams to embed a mutual learning operating style and to operate collaboratively through engaging in productive and effective conversations, it is crucial to master the following three mutual learning frameworks.

Framework #1: Left- and right-hand columns

There are four conversations happening simultaneously within every conversation:

1. What we are thinking and feeling and not saying

2. What we are saying

3. What the other party is thinking and feeling and not saying

4. What the other party is saying.

In the left-hand column, we have assessments, beliefs and opinions that influence and impact how we show up and participate in the conversation. The first step towards mastering a mutual learning operating style is to acknowledge your thoughts and know their potential impact. When we speak our minds and share unfiltered thoughts and feelings, we risk losing dignity and respect, and we exacerbate the problem. Only by speaking our truth and sharing what is important while holding others with respect and dignity are we more likely to move towards a mutually acceptable outcome.

In difficult conversations, it's essential to acknowledge one's thoughts and feelings. When we know our thoughts and feelings, we can decide what is important to bring into the conversation while holding the other person with respect, dignity and legitimacy. Difficult conversations are difficult because we *suppress* rather than *express* our left-hand column. Conversations become emotionally volatile when either or both parties 'illegitimise' their respective left-hand columns.

When we know what thoughts and feelings to bring into the conversation, we facilitate greater understanding. And only with greater understanding can we make more informed decisions and take wiser action.

To practise using this tool at your next meeting, take a piece of paper and draw a line down the middle. In the left-hand column capture the essence of the thoughts and feelings you're not sharing. In the right-hand column capture the essence of what is being said.

Framework #2: Balance advocacy and inquiry

Conversations happen in dialogue. No conversation can take place when one or both parties turn up to only speak.

> Advocate as if you are right.
> Inquire as if you are wrong.

A dialogue is an interactive process between at least two people who share ideas and perspectives and who invite others to share theirs. For there to be dialogue, both parties need to balance advocating their views and inquiring into the other's perspective. Rather than trying to be interesting, be interested.

Integral to collaborative teams is the quality of team members' conversations where they must each demonstrate high advocacy with high inquiry.

Balance Advocacy and Inquiry

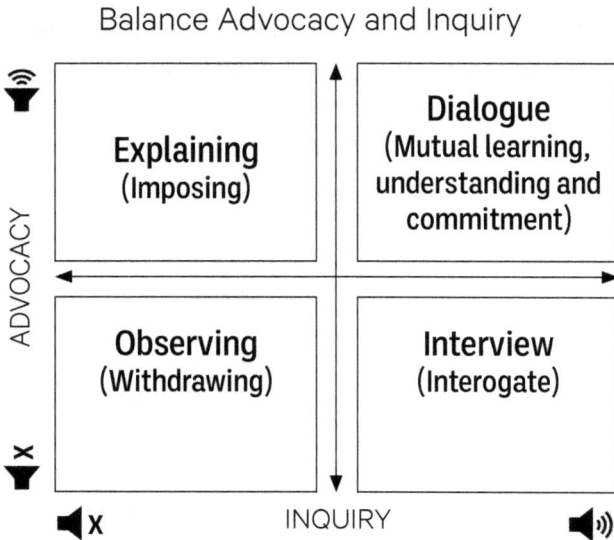

Team members who engage in high advocacy with low inquiry are described as 'imposing': all that matters and all that gets heard is what they think and believe. Conversely, team members who don't share what they think or feel (low advocacy) and who focus mostly on inquiring into others' thinking, are experienced as intimidating where others feel unsafe to share their views and respond in a guarded manner. But when no one shares what they are thinking, assumptions are made and this can have disastrous consequences.

The only way to create a space to learn with and from one another is for team members to show courage and confidence (high advocacy) and to ask rather than assume (high inquiry). Real learning, meaningful dialogue, deeper understanding and greater commitment is only possible by balancing high advocacy and high inquiry.

Framework #3: Conversations for Learning

Conversations for Learning are designed in four interdependent conversations:

1. Conversations for Clarity: intent and mutual benefit.

2. Conversations for Concern: advocate concerns.

3. Conversations for Understanding: inquire from others.

4. Conversations for Action: co-design action.

The diagram below shows four interdependent elements of Conversations for Learning and core mutual learning behaviours within each type of conversation.

Conversations for Learning

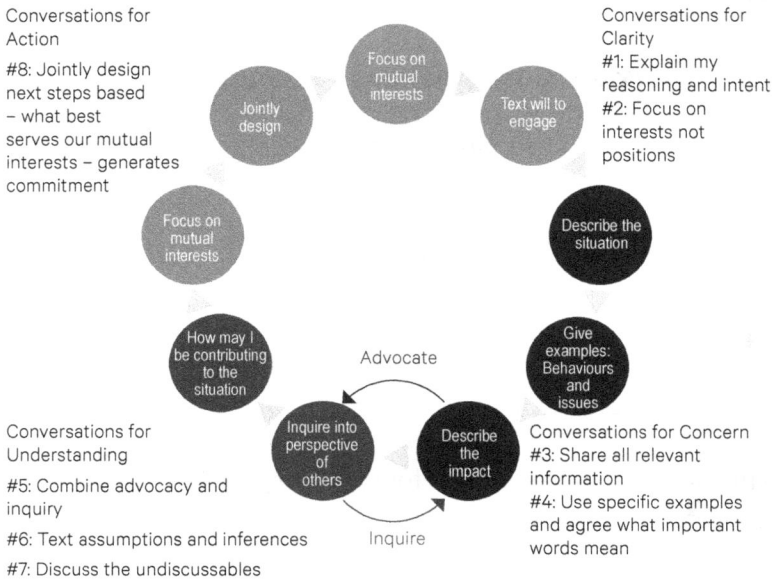

Conversations for Action
#8: Jointly design next steps based – what best serves our mutual interests – generates commitment

Conversations for Clarity
#1: Explain my reasoning and intent
#2: Focus on interests not positions

Conversations for Understanding
#5: Combine advocacy and inquiry
#6: Text assumptions and inferences
#7: Discuss the undiscussables

Conversations for Concern
#3: Share all relevant information
#4: Use specific examples and agree what important words mean

I invite you to look at the Conversations for Learning framework above as a process to guide 'difficult' conversations rather than prescribe how they ought to be managed. Difficult conversations require the space to evolve, flow and meander to elicit meaning, understanding and commitment. For this to happen, conversations need to be enhanced by and not restricted to a process. The four interdependent conversations bridge the parties' diverse views and perspectives to reach an aligned and committed outcome.

When difficult conversation gets derailed, it's because the parties start from their Conversations for Concern rather than their Conversations for Clarity. They start from their position, not from where they believe the mutual interests are and how they stand to mutually benefit from engaging in the conversation.

Let me illustrate how a 'difficult' conversation could be managed through the Conversations for Learning process. Assume you are concerned about your deteriorating working relationship with one of your colleagues and you seek to engage them in a conversation to address the problem and improve the relationship.

First, the Conversations for Clarity. It's crucial to start by framing the conversation through declaring your intentions— what you believe to be the mutual purpose and benefits of the conversation. It's important you don't assume that the other person views it the same way. Test whether they recognise there to be an issue and if so, how they see the mutual benefits of engaging with you to address it.

The Conversations for Clarity could start like this:

> 'I'd like to discuss an issue I feel is negatively impacting our relationship. If it's not addressed, I believe it will continue to make it difficult for us to work effectively together. I believe our ability to succeed and achieve what we have set out to achieve is dependent upon us building and maintaining an effective working relationship.'

Then follow up and inquire as to how they may see it. Ask them:

> 'How do you feel about having this conversation and working with me to address the issues, and finding a way we both feel will help to improve our relationship?'

If they don't think it's necessary to have the conversation or don't believe there is an issue in your working relationship, offer your differing perspective (remember, we see things differently). Share your belief and invite them to revisit the conversation at a later stage. Agree on a time to re-engage. Should they agree, however, go straight into the conversation.

The following list of questions will help in facilitating more effective Conversations for Learning and will enable you to master and embed a mutual learning operating style.

Conversations for Clarity (to reach a shared understanding of the intention and what and why the discussion is taking place):

1. What do we want to achieve from this conversation?

2. How will we know our time has been well spent?

3. What would be a valuable way to use this time?

4. What would we like to be different after our conversation?

5. What is important for you and me to discuss?

6. How realistic and achievable is the goal?

7. What does success look like to you?

8. What do you want to change or what will be different?

Second, the Conversations for Concern. Advocate (share) what is not going as well as you would like. Express how important it is to you. It's critical to give examples of what you mean. The Situation, Behaviour, Impact (S.B.I.) modelled within the Conversations for Learning model is a helpful tool in breaking down an example so that the other party understands what you mean. Here's how you could share your concern using the S.B.I. model.

Assume that in your left-hand column you have noted your fear of how they will react. Having observed this assessment, you bring it into the conversation. You could say something like:

'I find this difficult to talk about because I'm not sure how you will react. But let me give you an example of what I mean by our deteriorating relationship. At the meeting this morning, (Situation) you shared your views on the lack of progress on the project and went on to blame my team for what you felt was a lack of commitment (Behaviour). I must say, I found that to be highly inappropriate, and what's more, I questioned why you never raised this with me before the meeting. After the meeting, most of my team members questioned whether to trust you moving forward (Impact).'

The following list of questions will help in facilitating more effective Conversations for Learning and will enable you to master and embed a mutual learning operating style.

Conversations for Concern (to identify what's important that could be going better):

1. What is not going as well as it could for you?
2. How would you describe the current situation?
3. What is happening right now?
4. What assumptions are you making? How realistic are they?
5. What are some of the key factors?
6. What other factors are relevant?
7. What prevents you from achieving your goal?
8. What's working and what's not working for you?

9. What needs to change?

10. What's happening because of the present situation?

11. What is preventing you from achieving your goal?

12. Where would you like to start?

Invite them to tell you their story:

1. How does this happen?

2. When does this happen?

3. When did this issue become a problem for you?

4. How does this affect you?

Third, the Conversations for Understanding. Having advocated your concern, it's time to move the conversation on and invite the other person to share their perspectives. Inquire into how they heard what you have said and how they wish to respond. Inquire how they may have a different perspective. It's critical here that you listen intending to understand; it's not the time to respond or be defensive. During this phase of the conversation the parties 'dance' between balancing advocacy and inquiry. This is where learning and understanding happens—or not.

You could ask:

'I'd be keen to understand your perspective and to hear your response to what I've just said.'

Also, given that one of the mutual learning assumptions is that we may be contributing in ways we do not see, it's important to ask the question:

'Is there anything I might have said or done that led you to do and say what you did?'

The following list of questions will help in facilitating more effective Conversations for Learning and will enable you to master and embed a mutual learning operating style.

Conversations for Understanding (to explore a range of possibilities to address the concern):

1. What could you do in your current situation?
2. What new possibilities could you consider?
3. What is the most attractive option?
4. What are the advantages and disadvantages of this option?
5. What has worked for you in the past?
6. What have you tried so far?
7. How can you do more of what has worked for you?
8. What can be done to change the situation?
9. What should you do to make this happen?
10. Whose support would you need?
11. What could you do to change the situation?
12. Who might help?
13. Would you like a suggestion from me?
14. What option do you think is the best?
15. What are the pros and cons of your preferred option?
16. What do you see as the possibilities?

Fourth, the Conversations for Action. These are the actions to resolve the matter and achieve the mutual purpose and benefits for having the conversation that both parties commit to. Once both parties have advocated their concerns and inquired to ensure greater understanding of each other's perspectives, it is appropriate to jointly design a course of action that both parties accept and for which they are prepared to hold themselves accountable.

As we acknowledge, human behaviour is unpredictable by nature. No process is absolute. There are no predetermined outcomes. However, when engaging in difficult conversations, adopting a unilateral control approach will almost certainly lead to greater misunderstandings, more entrenched positions and escalated conflict.

The following list of questions will help in facilitating more effective Conversations for Learning and will enable you to master and embed a mutual learning operating style.

Conversations for Action (to identify the action they commit to take):

1. What are you going to now do to address this matter?
2. What are your next steps?
3. When will you take the next steps?
4. How confident are you that this will work?
5. What might get in your way? What may prevent you from achieving this outcome?
6. What will you do if these things prevent you from achieving your goal?

7. How will you know you have succeeded?

8. Whose support will you need?

9. How and when will you get the support?

10. When do you hope to have completed the actions?

11. When shall we meet to review your progress?

COMING UP IN PART SIX

Let's reflect on the content of this book. In Part One, we explored the inherent paradoxes in teams and that despite the power of teams, high performing teams are rare. Part Two highlighted the four types of teams and how they differ from one another based on the quality of their working relationships and the quality of their collective results.

In Parts Three and Four, we explored the 5 distinguishing Disciplines of High Performing Teams. Data collected over the past 10 years from teams I have worked with revealed that most teams flounder more than flourish. In Part Five, we covered the predominant operating style flourishing teams adopt and the frameworks to enable team members to significantly improve the quality of their conversations and working relationships.

Nothing changes until something changes. In Part Six, I will outline what a team coaching journey includes and the approach taken to help teams who may be floundering to transition to flourish and to operate at more than the sum of its parts, more often.

Part Six

Team coaching (program)

Team Coaching Program for high performing teams

Unlocking the power in teams and accessing the collective capacity and capability requires teams to embark on a transformational learning journey. The following Team Coaching Program overview provides an insight into the structure, methodology and content of the program as well as the benefits teams have derived from embarking on this learning journey.

PROGRAM OBJECTIVES

To enable the leadership team to improve its collective performance by working better together and achieve those performance goals that can be achieved only by working more interdependently.

The more specific objectives include:

- To enable the team to better understand and deliver on its mandate from stakeholders.

- To establish a sense of purpose and secure greater levels of commitment and cooperation across the team to achieve common performance goals and outcomes.

- To improve the quality of the working relationships and build greater trust-based relationships.

- To facilitate greater levels of understanding and make more informed decisions by respecting and legitimising others' diverse perspectives and opinions.

- To create a 'learning system' and increase the team's collective capacity and capability to achieve better results.

- To create a safe environment for team members to address and resolve conflicts, speak more of their truth and discuss the undiscussables.

PROGRAM CONTENT

To achieve the above objectives and ensure the team collectively demonstrates lasting positive behavioural change, the program content embeds the following 5 Disciplines that distinguish high performing teams:

Discipline #1: Discover our Mandate

What our stakeholders require from and of us

To align the team members' understanding of what their key stakeholders have commissioned the team with. In addition, to ensure team members are committed and own the learning experience. It is important that team members share their perspectives of how they feel and experience being part of the team and to also contribute towards creating a vision of what success looks like for the team.

Approach for Discipline to Discover:

Part One: Discovery conversations

As facilitator, to meet with each team member to discuss, capture and provide feedback to the team a summary of their perspectives on:

- Who does the team serve? Who are the key stakeholders?

- What does each stakeholder appreciate, find difficult and want different from the team going forward?

- What is the team's unique contribution to meeting the organisation's future needs?

- What prevents the team from achieving the levels of excellence for which it strives?

- To be a high performing team, what needs to be different in how the team operates?

Part Two: Assessment of the 5 Disciplines of High Performing Teams

The team members complete the *5 Disciplines of High Performing Teams Assessment* based on how they experience and perceive the team. Opportunities will be made available four months post-program to reassess the team and determine the shifts and behavioural changes made.

Part Three: Individual learning priorities

Each team member will have the opportunity to identify what is most important for them to commit to learning more about and to change from participating in the program. The identified learning priorities anchor the learning from the program and progress will be continuously reviewed during the program.

Discipline #2: Declare our Purpose

What the team is for

A team succeeds by committing to a unifying purpose—an uncompromising commitment to 'why' the team exists and the cause it serves that is greater than itself. High performing teams start from their 'why'.

Approach for Discipline to Declare:

To come together as a team and align understanding on:

1. The team's value: the difference it makes to its stakeholders.
2. The team's purpose: the cause it serves that's greater than itself.
3. What the team stands for: its values.

Discipline #3: Design our Culture

How team members engage and relate

Teams rise and fall based on the strength of their working relationships. Relationships and conversations are the lifeblood of effective teamwork. Conversations that do not generate new insights, innovative practices, effective actions and positive results are unproductive, and they create and perpetuate costly communication breakdowns and waste.

Approach for Discipline to Design:

To identify, commit and be held accountable:

1. For the 'ways of working' team members uncompromisingly commit to uphold when they engage and relate, together and apart.
2. To build and maintain effective working relationships based on these elements:

   RESPECT: afforded to diverse and similar views and perspectives.

   TRUST: placed in themselves and others.

CONCERNS: an appreciation of what is important to each team member.

MOODS: to live and lead from resourceful moods that best serve all.

APPRECIATION: of perspectives, capability and contribution each brings.

ALIGNMENT: in the direction the team is moving and how it might get there.

COORDINATION OF ACTION: by securing greater cooperation and commitment.

QUALITY OF CONVERSATIONS: the ability to feel safe to speak one's truth.

3. To understand the impact team members' assumptions and assessments have on the quality of conversations that may contribute to 'wasteful' interpersonal interaction.

4. To employ conversational approaches that enable team members to effectively address conflict and make it possible to constructively discuss the undiscussables.

5. To appreciate how the moods in the team impact others and to shift the moods to enable greater levels of commitment and cooperation to achieve desired outcomes.

6. To adopt an operating style that enables team members to better understand each other, make more informed decisions together and secure greater commitment

and accountability to the team's collective performance goals.

Discipline #4: Deliver our Results

Achieve the team's collective performance goals

Teams are about getting things done—getting results. Only through teamwork can people interact to ensure work flows smoothly to the satisfactory completion of what is required. For work to flow smoothly, it requires team members to coordinate action together through securing one another's cooperation and commitment. Teams are about achieving outcomes no one individual can achieve working independently.

Approach for Discipline to Deliver:

As a team, learn how to achieve better outcomes through securing greater levels of commitment and cooperation from one another and across the organisation.

1. How to discern between bad, good and great work performed by the team.

2. How to identify the team's collective performance goals that can only be achieved by working interdependently.

3. How to coordinate action through securing greater levels of cooperation and commitment.

4. How to make meetings matter and deliver more great work.

Discipline #5: Develop our Learning

Grow and develop the collective capacity

Teams are living systems, continuously learning and evolving into more than the sum of their parts. High performing teams are committed to supporting and developing the learning and performance of every team member. Collective and individual learning are interdependent.

Approach for Discipline to Develop:

As a team, learn how to:

    a.   Give, receive and learn from feedback and feedforward.

    b.   Appreciate that we can't change what we can't see, and learn to be different observers of ourselves and others so new possibilities become accessible.

    c.   Be open to asking for help and support and to offer others help and support.

    d.   Recognise successes and failures, and build a learning culture.

PROGRAM STRUCTURE

To enable the team to evolve to become a high performing team and embed lasting positive behavioural change, the program structure includes these interdependent components:

1. Discovery Phase

2. Leadership Team Workshops

3. Peer Action-Learning Groups

4. Executive Coaching: Team Leader

5. In-Team Coaching: Leadership Team

6. Return on Learning Experience (R.O.L.E.)

Component 1: Discovery phase

To identify team members' perspectives of how they feel and experience being part of the team, to contribute towards creating a vision of what success looks like for the team, and to secure their understanding and commitment to the program.

Component 2: Leadership team workshops

The team workshops embed the 5 Disciplines of a Smart Team and reinforce a common understanding of the team's guiding principles, mindset, commitments and skills that underpin the team's 'teaming way'. Before each team workshop, team members will have to complete some reading and tasks (pre-work). The pre-work is important as it ensures that everyone is prepared to contribute to a valuable learning experience.

Each team workshop comprises discussions, sub-group exercises, practise, case studies and other facilitative processes to enable team members to be different observers and identify new possibilities to adapting their thinking and behaviour to achieve better outcomes. After each team workshop, team members will reflect and commit to a plan of action to implement their learning. This is reviewed in the peer action-learning groups.

Component 3: Peer action-learning groups

The peer action-learning groups are vital to achieving sustained behavioural change. It is often the element that ensures the transition from learning and intent into practical implementation and sustained behavioural change.

The peer action-learning groups comprise groups of three to four team members who meet within two weeks following each team workshop. Their primary purpose is to ensure that each team member holds themselves and their peers accountable for implementing their commitments and action plans identified during the team workshops and to share their progress in addressing their individual learning priorities.

The peer action-learning groups provide the added benefit of building closer working relationships among peers. Through developing greater understanding of each other and working together to develop strategies to deal with challenges and concerns, team members make better quality decisions implemented more quickly and effectively.

Component 4: Executive coaching: team leader

To ensure maximum value and benefits are derived from the learning experience, the team leader can participate in a 1:1 executive coaching program to support them in facilitating desired behavioural changes important to them and the team.

The executive coaching program offers the following features:

a. The coaching program will run concurrently for six months plus a further six months after completing the program. This will enable the leader to sustain their own and the team's collective learning momentum to facilitate lasting positive behavioural change.

b. The leader can participate in The Leadership Circle 360 assessment: a critical component to the learning is to get feedback at the outset and upon completion of the coaching program to assess the impact and benefits of the behavioural change.

c. In addition, third-party feedback will be collected and provided to assess and evaluate the impact of the behaviour changes and where further opportunities for learning and improvement may present.

Component 5: In-team coaching: leadership team

To realise the return from the learning experience and embed lasting positive behavioural change, opportunity will be provided for the facilitator to attend four leadership team meetings to observe and provide feedback on how effectively the learning is applied to real matters in real time. This is a core component to facilitating collective learning and scaling the collective capacity and capability of the team.

Component 6: Assess the return on learning experience (R.O.L.E.)

Three to four months post-program, the team will come together for a one-day workshop to assess the return on the learning experience (R.O.L.E.). This will include a reassessment of the team against the 5 Disciplines of High Performing Teams, assessing success against the program objectives, the individual and collective learning commitments and stakeholder feedback. Most important, this workshop will serve as an opportunity to identify ongoing learning priorities and modes of learning to sustain the positive behavioural changes.

BENEFITS FROM THE TEAM COACHING PROGRAM

Teams who have participated in the Team Coaching Program have claimed these benefits:

1. We spend half the time and energy focused on reacting to tactical issues.

2. We have doubled our time and energy to addressing the strategic and transformational imperatives.

3. We have doubled the level of trust team members have in each other.

4. Less time is wasted in unproductive meetings.

5. We have doubled the level of productivity and quality of output from team meetings.

6. There are no undiscussables.

7. There is 100% improvement in the levels of safety team members feel to speak their truth—twice as much is spoken.

8. The team operates at more than the sum of its parts for more of the time; it is flourishing more than floundering.

9. We have doubled our levels of team member engagement.

10. Team achievements are recognised more than individual accomplishments.

CONCLUSION

My intention in writing this book was to show how possible it is to take what we know to be common sense about teams and make it common practice. In the world of work, whether teaming together or apart, teams will always achieve what no other entity can.

The 5 Disciplines of High Performing Teams go to the essence of what distinguishes high performing teams and what it takes to flourish and perform at more than the sum of its parts for more of the time. Transitioning to become a flourishing team requires a commitment to engaging in a learning experience—in-team coaching. Team coaching is growing fast and will continue to do so because of what Peter Hawkins claims as the three driving forces:

1. The increasing need for more shared and collective leadership in an increasingly complex and interconnected world of work.

2. Team-working is increasingly a major competitive advantage given the increasing necessity for organisations to do more and be better and with less resources.

3. The power of teams to coordinate action and integrate across functions, sectors, cultures and countries.

As leaders, we have the responsibility to create organisations fit for the future. This requires us to cultivate a culture of teamwork where the leadership team 'teams better together' and where all teams across the organisation become a team of teams.

The first step in transitioning to become a collaborative, high performing team is to assess where the team is now. As part of the discovery phase and before commencing the Team Coaching Program, we assess the team against the 5 Disciplines and capture each team member's insights into what it feels like to be part of the team and what they believe to be the team's strengths, challenges and opportunities.

To know more about how your team and organisation could benefit from engaging in my Team Coaching Program, and to take the first step by assessing the team against the 5 Disciplines, contact Bernard Desmidt by email at bernard@ bernarddesmidt.com or by phone on +61 (0)414 654 437.

Nothing changes until something changes. As the next step, take the next step.

REFERENCES

2019 Edelman Trust Barometer. (2019, January 20). Edelman. https://www.edelman.com/trust/2019-trust-barometer

Brooks, D. (2020). *The Second Mountain: The Quest for a Moral Life.* Random House Trade Paperbacks.

Dunning, D. (2012). *Self-Insight: Roadblocks and Detours on the Path to Knowing Thyself* (1st ed.). Psychology Press.

Geus, A. D. (1999). *The Living Company: Growth, Learning and Longevity in Business.* Nicholas Brealey Publishing.

Hackman, J. R. (2002). *Leading Teams: Setting the Stage for Great Performances* (1st ed.). Harvard Business Review Press.

Hawkins, P. (2021). *Leadership Team Coaching: Developing Collective Transformational Leadership* (4th ed.). Kogan Page.

Heen, S., & Stone, D. (2019, March 19). *Find the Coaching in Criticism.* Harvard Business Review. https://hbr.org/2014/01/find-the-coaching-in-criticism

Katzenbach, J., Smith, D. (2015). *The Wisdom of Teams: Creating the High-Performance Organization.* HarperBusiness.

Kofman, F., Wilber, K., & Senge, P. (2013). *Conscious Business: How to Build Value through Values* (Reprint ed.). Sounds True.

Lencioni, P. (2002). *The Five Dysfunctions of a Team: A Leadership Fable* (1st ed.). Jossey-Bass.

Maister, D. H., Galford, R., & Green, C. (2021). *The Trusted Advisor: 20th Anniversary Edition* (Anniversary ed.). Free Press.

Mourkogiannis, N. (2008). *Purpose: The Starting Point of Great Companies* (Reprint ed.). St. Martin's Griffin.

Perlow, L., Hadley, C., & Eun, E. (2017, June 26). *Stop the Meeting Madness*. Harvard Business Review. https://hbr.org/2017/07/stop-the-meeting-madness

Pink, D. H. (2011). *Drive: The Surprising Truth About What Motivates Us*. Riverhead Books.

Rabey, G. (2003). *The Paradox of Teamwork*. Industrial and Commercial Training (Vol. 35). MCB UP Ltd. https://www.emerald.com/insight/content/doi/10.1108/00197850310479141/full/html

Schwarz, R. M. (2013). *Smart Leaders, Smarter Teams: How You and Your Team Get Unstuck to Get Results* (1st ed.). Jossey-Bass.

Searle, J. R. (1969). *Speech Acts*. Cambridge Core. https://www.cambridge.org/core/books/speech-acts/D2D7B03E472C8A390ED60B86E08640E7

Senge, P. M. (2006). *The Fifth Discipline: The Art and Practice of the Learning Organization*. Image Books.

Sieler, A. (n.d.). *Coaching to the Human Soul Volume III: The Biological and Somatic Basis of Ontological Coaching*. Newfield Australia.

Stanier, B. M., Godin, S., Babauta, L., Guillebeau, C., Port, M., & Ulrich, D. (2010a). *Do More Great Work: Stop the Busywork. Start the Work That Matters*. (Illustrated ed.). Workman Publishing Company.

Ury, W., Fisher, R., & Patton, B. (2012). *Getting to Yes: Negotiating Agreement Without Giving In*. Random House.

Wageman, R., Nunes, D., Burruss, J., & Hackman, J. R. (2008). *Senior Leadership Teams: What It Takes to Make Them Great* (First Edition). Harvard Business Review Press.

www.ingramcontent.com/pod-product-compliance
Lightning Source LLC
Chambersburg PA
CBHW071545200326
41519CB00021BB/6618